NORTH TO KATAHDIN

Also by Eric Pinder

Life at the Top
Tying Down the Wind

NORTH TO

KATAHDIN

Eric Pinder

MILKWEED EDITIONS

Published 2005 by Milkweed Editions
Printed in the United States of America
Cover design by Kyle Hunter
Cover photo by Eric Pinder
Author photo by Meg Barthelman
Interior design by Rachel Holscher
The text of this book is set in Jenson Pro.
13 14 15 16 17   5 4 3 2
First Edition

Milkweed Editions, a nonprofit publisher, gratefully acknowledges support from
Emilie and Henry Buchwald; Bush Foundation; Cargill Value Investment; Timothy
and Tara Clark Family Charitable Fund; DeL Corazón Family Fund; Dougherty
Family Foundation; Ecolab Foundation; Joe B. Foster Family Foundation; General
Mills Foundation; Jerome Foundation; Kathleen Jones; Constance B. Kunin; D. K.
Light; Chris and Ann Malecek; McKnight Foundation; a grant from the Minnesota
State Arts Board, through an appropriation by the Minnesota State Legislature, a grant
from the National Endowment for the Arts, and private funders; Sheila C. Morgan;
Laura Jane Musser Fund; an award from the National Endowment for the Arts, which
believes that a great nation deserves great art; Navarre Corporation; Kate and Stuart
Nielsen; Outagamie Charitable Foundation; Qwest Foundation; Debbie Reynolds;
St. Paul Travelers Foundation; Ellen and Sheldon Sturgis; Surdna Foundation; Target
Foundation; Gertrude Sexton Thompson Charitable Trust (George R. A. Johnson,
Trustee); James R. Thorpe Foundation; Toro Foundation; Weyerhaeuser Family
Foundation; and Xcel Energy Foundation.

Library of Congress Cataloging-in-Publication Data

Pinder, Eric, 1970–
    North to Katahdin / Eric Pinder.
       p. cm.
    Includes bibliographical references.
    ISBN-13: 978-1-57131-280-8 (pbk. : alk. paper)
    ISBN-10: 1-57131-280-3
    1. Hiking—Maine—Katahdin, Mount. 2. Katahdin, Mount (Me.)—Description
and travel. 3. Wilderness areas—Maine. I. Title.
    GV199.42.M2P56 2005
    796.51'09741'3—dc22
                                                              2004027345

for Sarah and Tim

I owe thanks to the many people who read and commented on various drafts of the manuscript, notably Barbara Shor, David Smith, Ken Hoffman, Barry O'Connell, Jennifer Morin, Sarah Long, Meg Barthelman, my agent Laura Langlie, and H. Emerson Blake at Milkweed. Jean Hoekwater, Heather Haskell, and the rangers at Baxter State Park shared their knowledge and experiences, as did Peter Crane at the Mount Washington Observatory. Thanks are due to Appalachian Trail hikers Steve Piotrow, Bryan Yeaton, and Dick Bailey. Thanks also to my parents and my grandmother, for introducing me to Katahdin, and to Jennifer Paigen, for sharing the trail.

NORTH TO KATAHDIN

Everything looks different in the clouds.
You think you see a man and he turns out to be only a rock.
It kind of scares a fellow.

DONN FENDLER, *Lost on a Mountain in Maine*

NORTH TO KATAHDIN

Travelers

On the thirty-first of August, 1846, an early morning train stopped in Concord, Massachusetts, where it was boarded by a small, gaunt man who sometimes made pencils for a living. A sightseer of sorts, the man took a seat, nodded his chin to his chest, and promptly fell asleep. An hour later, in Boston, he woke from his nap to switch trains, now headed for Portland, Maine, then by steamboat to Bangor, where he boarded a stagecoach to the distant town of Mattawamkeag. There, all roads ended, and his journey began in earnest.

Mattawamkeag was a frontier town, a gateway to the Great North Woods. Beyond it, a land of trees, rivers, moose, and bears stretched across the horizon to the Canadian line. Mount Katahdin, the seventh highest mountain in New England,* stood thirty-five roadless

---

* Peak-baggers would call it the sixth highest, omitting 5,533-foot Mount Clay in New Hampshire. Peak-bagging is the hobby of hiking or climbing predetermined

3

miles to the northwest, deep in the wooded core of Maine—a great granite dome protruding abruptly from the evergreen forest. The man intended to scale this mountain, but he would not succeed.

It was not for pencils or for mountain climbing that the young Massachusetts man was best known; it was for oddity. When he was not earning a living as a pencil maker, he was simply living— and living simply. His name was Henry David Thoreau, and it was the end of the second summer of his experiment in loneliness at Walden Pond, which would one day make him famous.[†] Thoreau had sold a summer's worth of beans, bought a ticket to Bangor, and rode, walked, and paddled the rest of the way to the mountain along the Penobscot River. Within a week he stood on a rocky shoulder of land less than a mile from Katahdin's summit. Clumps of brownish green diapensia plants, stranded on the mountaintop during the last ice age, squatted at his feet; tiny arctic spiders crawled under the rocks.

Something there daunted Thoreau. Perhaps it was the barren and treeless granite landscape, the wind, or the "unhandselled and ancient" visage of nature mentioned in his journal. He turned and fled, never to reach the highest peak.

---

lists of peaks, such as New England's "Highest Hundred" or the tallest peak in each of the fifty United States or, more ambitiously, the "Seven Summits"—the highest mountain on each continent. Mount Clay is too easily accessible from a ridgeline connecting it to its neighbors Mount Washington and Mount Jefferson to be considered a peak worth "bagging" on its own. So it appears only on maps, not on peak-baggers' lists. Who knows what sort of peak-bagger Thoreau might have become with an automobile and an interstate highway system at his disposal? As it was, he preferred to visit a few favorite places multiple times. Nineteenth-century transportation prevented him from indulging in this sort of shopping-list approach to mountains.

[†] Thoreau wasn't a complete recluse at Walden. His cabin contained three chairs, and those chairs occasionally contained visitors. In his own words, "I had three chairs in my house; one for solitude, two for friendship, three for society."

When I first tried to read Thoreau, I was just eight years old, staying with my grandmother in Millinocket, Maine, with a view of Katahdin from my bedroom window. One morning, clouds swirled over the summit, swept east by the wind, stirring darkness and cold air in the skies over town. I took a book from the shelf, wrapped myself in a blanket, and read.

Reading *The Maine Woods* served as a prelude to hiking in it, for the very next day I was going to go there, to Katahdin, the cloud maker. But the writing proved too difficult for an eight-year-old. I grew impatient with Thoreau's narration; for seventy-odd pages he wades in rivers, talking to lumberjacks and Indians. I wanted him to get to the grim, gray mountain looming over Millinocket in the north, that monolith I saw outside my window. By sunset I had given up Thoreau. Then it was morning; time to go.

For three days the sky precipitated a cold, misty drizzle. Ghostly waves of fog sifted through the woods. The summit, thrust deep into the belly of a cloud, was impossible to see. In a cabin at the base of the mountain, with little to do, I learned to play poker with my father and two strangers. A fire crackled in the woodstove. Its heat steamed the single window, melting the frost. Shadows of flame danced on the adjacent wall.

I remember the time as autumn, but I know now it must have been May, the last month of one of those brisk, lingering winters that used to torment New England. Rain tapped gently against a tin roof, lulling me back to sleep.

The mountain didn't seem crowded that year. Only twelve people fit in the cabin— and because of the rain I saw no one else—but records indicate thousands of people were stomping their hiking boots in the spring mud. Nor was Katahdin the only destination. In the White Mountains, the Smokies, the Rockies, Yosemite, and Yellowstone, millions more parked their cars and pitched their tents. Ever since, the number of outdoor recreation seekers has only increased. Crowds now gather at the trailheads.

In 1846 Thoreau said of mountains like Katahdin, "It will be a long time before the tide of fashionable travel sets that way."

That time is now.

How would Thoreau adapt to such a change? Clearly marked, well-worn paths through the woods plus modern campground accommodations, Global Positioning Satellite units and other high-tech hiking gear would surely startle Thoreau if he could hike Katahdin again today. But mostly he'd be shocked at the once unthinkable number of people who'd want to join him on the trail.

Before Thoreau, only a very few people had climbed or tried to climb a mountain. Those who did—scientists, surveyors, and loggers—had legitimate, money-making reasons. But Thoreau was Katahdin's first tourist. He had no particular reason or need to ascend a mountain. He simply wanted to do it.

I want to know why. Why bother to go to mountains at all? Mountains reward climbers with sore legs and weary arms. Rocks tear holes in the soles of their shoes, while mooseflies and mosquitoes busily extract a blood toll. Thoreau could just as easily have worn out his boots walking in the woods near Concord. Instead, he chose Katahdin, a long and difficult journey to the north. What was he seeking?

More than a century and a half since Thoreau's partial ascent, people have followed him by the millions up steep alpine walls to Katahdin and perhaps also to Kilimanjaro and Everest. Even in the two decades since my own childhood visits to Katahdin, I've noticed a change. Familiar footpaths are worn wider, trod upon by an increasing number of feet. For the first time in history, mountains have become outdoor playgrounds, granite jungle gyms, popular among those seeking an escape from work, stress, home.

I want to discover what draws people to the lands above the trees, but I will not climb Katahdin—not yet. A lesser peak will satisfy. Like Thoreau, the guru of Concord, I intend to look *at* the mountain, not off it. It's better to start in the forest, to drink from icy brooks that flow off the peaks, to stand on a nearby hill and gaze at the mountain from afar.

The hill is called Traveler Mountain, or sometimes just "the Traveler." It stands little more than 3,500 feet tall, but that is enough elevation to possess a timberline. For an hour I have sat on a boulder on the barren Peak of the Ridges and shared the view with a bumblebee. A true mountain, Katahdin, rears into the sky fifteen miles south of here, but my eye focuses on the bee. It's large but drably colored like the rock on which it perches—rhyolite, an igneous rock, cool to the touch, gray in color but spiced with white quartz and feldspar. On the rock's surface, the bee is curled like a comma, its translucent wings twitching in the wind. Long and lean, the bee sits on its lump of smooth rhyolite two feet away, washing the sticks of its legs, over and over. It refuses to move away.

Earlier this morning, at the head of the Pogy Notch Trail, I left behind a warm summer day and climbed up, over, and around five miles of boulders into the brisk winds of late November. Down below it is July. Like the bee, I now huddle against a slab of rock, frozen by gusts out of Canada. The bee has the advantage. It is protected by a niche in the rock. An inch above its tiny body blows a gale that could whisk it away like a scrap of paper.

Why is the bee here in this flowerless gray place? Why does it stay? Maybe it was carried on the wind, tossed through the air until it found refuge on the leeward side of a rock.

I have no such excuse. I deliberately hiked the first mile and a half of the narrow Pogy Notch Trail to where a branch trail led steeply up the slopes. Far below me, that solitary footpath continues, winding south past Traveler Mountain into the shady heart of a two-hundred-thousand-acre wildlife refuge. Not long ago the forest to which the trail leads teemed with trucks and loggers. Now it's roadless, seemingly deserted. A thick growth of trees—hardwoods and firs—blocks off the horizon. The tallest trees are crowned with a canopy of twisted branches, and sunlight pours through a screen of twigs, scattering droplets of light on the dark ground below. Tiny saplings stand weakly in the shadows of these giants, and spread along the trail like a library of rough scrolls lie peelings of birch bark.

From my high ridge on Traveler Mountain I can spot an empty section of the trail, barely visible in the woods far below, where it runs alongside a brook. Trees crowd along the stream's banks and spread branches thinly over the water, creating a break in the canopy. From above, the trail looks like a narrow scar in the woods. Few go there, and no one comes to stay. People pass through quickly, as strangers, curious and observant but far from home. When they leave, bits of the forest go with them. In some thirsty hiker's belly rests a cold mouthful of South Branch Pond. Others take away specks of root on their boots or a fern frond pressed between the pages of a naturalist's notebook. Some take a leaf, a handful of berries, a glimpse of dark moose hide deep in the trees. Such are the delights of the journey, a day spent following brook waters down to a campground, where people more comfortably belong.

The bee has begun to watch me, or perhaps it senses the juice of the apple in my hand. In this jacket I am a bright blue target, the most flowerlike patch of color on a plateau of gray stone. I position myself upwind; if the bee wants to get me, it will have to work for it.

Strong and fresh, the wind pours down out of Quebec and northern Maine, unobstructed by any higher hills. A cloud spreads across the miles between Katahdin and my lonely perch on the Traveler. The moving cloud's shadow smothers the trees in a sudden darkness but behind it races a wake of fresh light. Other shadows lunge at Traveler Mountain, one by one, chasing after the shaggy clouds. They slide smoothly over the rocks, roll through ravines, and surge abruptly up the mountain's steep banks, gliding south toward Katahdin.

I face into the wind. The view north, away from the sun, shows a flat, green land spotted with lakes, hill-less and seemingly unoccupied by humanity. Civilization is behind me, creeping north along the rivers and lakes. Yet somewhere in the dense, green growth hundreds of miles of logging roads crisscross strips of denuded, unprotected land just outside the boundaries of Baxter State Park, the largest state park in Maine. In time, some architect from the overpopulated south, hungry for open space, will place a city there. But for now the land remains green and pristine, occasionally harvested for its trees.

A different scene exists to the south, where Pogy Notch Trail plunges through a lowland, bordered to the west by the deep waters of Wassataquoik Lake and a range of peaks named Sable, Lord, and Pogy. The view due south stops abruptly at a sheer wall six miles wide. There, the ground heaves itself up into the massive bulk of Mount Katahdin. Off the flanks of this titan roll high hills—Turner, Russell, Mullen—with still taller hills peeking over their shoulders.

Katahdin—spelled *Ktaadn* by Thoreau—is said to mean "greatest mountain" in the language of the Abenaki Indians. Sometimes it is translated as "highest land" or even "the big hill." It is certainly the biggest hill between here and the horizon, a mile-high wall of rock. Beyond this rampart the world ends. A smokestack, civilization's beacon, fumes in Millinocket, not twenty miles south, but from here it's invisible. The Atlantic Ocean could hurl itself against the southern slopes of that blue ridge, and no one in the north would know. Only ravens, eagles, and other birds, if they fly high enough, can see beyond Katahdin.

Not a single bird has flown past today. But I often have seen them flung across the sky by winds at great heights, swerving to control where the gusts take them. No other creatures are here on the Traveler except a few mosquitoes, soon swept away. In any case, I am suitably wrapped and cowled in three layers of clothing—weak protection from the chill breeze, but a suitable deterrent to bug bites. So far the bee has honored our truce.

The wind, which has been taciturn and stubborn all day, suddenly starts to whisper words. Voices carry upward and two shapes appear, a man and a woman. What causes them to struggle up these slopes, to rub their palms raw on a mad hands-and-feet scramble over gritty boulders, only to reach some high place from which they can only come down? What is so inherently pleasurable in a fierce gust of wind, that I face into it and am chilled in the hottest month of summer?

The two hikers stagger to the top, dressed lightly for the summery weather below. They are still warmed by the effort of the climb, but soon they will begin to feel the wind. With a shiver, the man reaches for his pack and pulls out a wool cap. He asks me to "do the touristy thing," and poses with his wife in front of a signpost, to remind them both years later where they have gone. They stand perilously close to the bee, but do not see the insect. She coils a slender, sunburned arm around his waist, while the man crafts a smile under the shadow of his moustache. I take their picture.

Three is enough of a crowd to make us all uncomfortable. They go on ahead a few yards, behind a slab of rock, to eat their lunch. I take the hint and leave, my time expired. It's rare in the height of the summer tourist season to find a mountaintop all to oneself. I'm grateful for my hour. Now it's their turn. I head downslope, back into July. In a few weeks they will look at that photograph and remember the rocks, the cold, the view. In a corner of the picture, if they look carefully enough, they will find a tiny bee huddling against a rock.

Black Cat's Cradle

It isn't often that I rise before the sun. A sudden noise has awakened me—a loon's cry. I open my eyes.

The sky is still black, but I can see the silhouette of Traveler Mountain blocking the stars east of my campground. To the south and west, fog obscures the sky.

Sleeping in the open air always refreshes me somehow, no matter if I've slept for one hour or nine. And a busy day demands an early start. I prop myself up on my elbows and breathe deeply. The sharp scent of pine needles saturates the air. I roll up the sleeping bag, stretch my arms, grab my hiking boots, and stroll down toward the water of South Branch Pond.

Steam rises off the pond and twists around the branches of birch, spruce, and hemlock. I stand submerged like the forest itself in a sea of mist. The pond water gurgles and slaps at the polished stones by my feet, but the rippled surface of South Branch Pond is hidden. The trees sleep. Swayed by wind, a million birch leaves twitch and flutter like the eyelids of dreamers.

Above me, a sliver of waning moon slices through streams of cirrus clouds racing across the eastern sky. In the north, constellations spin laggardly around Polaris. A dipper pours clouds into the pine groves of Maine; Taurus the Bull steps over a shoulder of eastern hills, pursued by the hunter Orion and the first chill of autumn. Closer, behind me, the cabins of a public campground have vanished in mist, silent in the twilight before dawn.

Soon I hear a Canada jay scratch dirt, digging for breakfast. A sparrow perched on a twig trills melodies. Two chipmunks chatter in their throats and start to scrounge for food at the base of a tree. Morning breezes sway the branches; they creak and moan, stretch and yawn.

Deep in the grass, the undercurrent of crickets dissipates. A jumping fish plops a single note on the surface of the pond. It's as if a voice has said, "Let there be light!" and added as an afterthought, "Let there be music, let there be a thawing of ground, a diffusion of life."

As the sun's red rays touch the mist, the forest awakens. The distant cry of a loon ripples through a layer of moist, early morning air. Somewhere, behind rows of birches, the loon's mate answers.

For an instant, the breezes stop rustling leaves. Chipmunks pause in their chatter and freeze. A moose deep in the woods, crossing the Pogy Notch Trail, stands with one hoof an inch off the ground, waiting for that shimmer of sound to end before he completes his step. All the forest is still.

Back in 1857, when Henry David Thoreau first tried to reduce the loon's cry to letters on a page, the result was an inadequate *hoo-hoo-ooo*. No later writer has done any better. "I could lie awake for hours listening to it, it is so thrilling," Thoreau wrote. "When this note is first heard very far off at midnight, you conclude that it is a pack of wolves baying the moon." Obviously onomatopoeia and metaphor are weak substitutes for the throat of a loon.

I've seen two burly, six-foot tourists from Boston suddenly stand like statues on the shore of South Branch Pond, paralyzed by loons. With one hand apiece gripping a canoe, the other warding off bugs, the two men had grunted, toting their boat toward the water. Then the loon sounded.

For an instant, the canoe is motionless in their arms. Mouths hang open in surprise. One man, in midswat, spares the life of a moosefly sucking blood off his cheek; even the fly pauses in mid-sip. Seconds later, he squashes it dead. The spell is broken. Canoe splashes in pond. Life continues.

Four of the sleek, black-and-white birds now settle on the pond, tiny dots bobbing on distant, golden water. The rhyolitic crags of Traveler Mountain wall in the pond to the east. On the western shore, a lumpy hill called Black Cat completes the valley. Waves of hardwood-dappled hills tumble south toward Mount Katahdin.

Black Cat is, perhaps, one of the least-climbed mountains in all the Appalachian Range. A single muddy trail runs to its crest where a weather-beaten, faintly brown-stained sign labels the hill "South Branch Mountain." Down below, a second wooden sign announces the start of the trail.

This sign stands mockingly on the far side of an outlet of South Branch Pond, a tiny brook pouring north toward Lake Matagamon in cold, clear gulps. I see no bridges here, no vines or ropes for swinging across, no hope of keeping dry. The soft, hissing water glides over boulders. No brook is likely to stop for the sake of one backpacker's dry feet.

I glance over the brook at the sign. I look from water to sign, from sign to water. How does anyone cross this? Water, sign, water—then

down at my forty-dollar nonwaterproof boots, the cheapest pair offered by L. L. Bean & Company. My white cotton socks are also
products of Freeport, Maine, Inc.

"Cotton kills," a friend had warned me when I left Millinocket
for the mountains two mornings ago. Wet cotton kills, she meant,
by inducing shivers and shakes. The evil fabric clings to the skin like
an eel, sucking out warmth and life. I wore it anyway.

"You're a fool," my friend added. Suddenly, I agree. As I risk a
step forward, pond water sweats and squishes through the pores in
my boots. Behind me, a moist footprint lingers in the mud.

Gingerly I slosh across and start up the mountain. A liter of lake
squeezes out of my boots with every forward step.

The planet, a scenic treadmill, rolls under me. Hikers, walkers, and
crawlers of all shapes and sizes have the strength to spin the earth.
A squirrel leaping from a birch tree to an elm sends the birch flying away behind it; the birch's trunk and roots, sunk deep in soil,
turn the world. The squirrel hovers in empty air, stationary, while
the elm tree flies closer.

A half-ton moose leans its bulk on its hind feet, and the earth
tumbles backward. A hawk launches into flight, kicking back a pine
tree; with it, the forests of Maine are flung east.

I do not weigh half a ton. I do not fly. But with every step across
this rocky stretch of four-hundred-million-year-old rhyolite, I roll
the globe beneath my feet, pushing back with my heels. This is a
heavy planet.

No wonder hikers build such strong legs; rolling a planet is hard
work. I stop, slip a canteen off my shoulder, gulp down a few swallows of South Branch Pond. I'll try now to spin the summit a little
closer, send the green arc of horizon whirling away behind me.

Soon the mists begin to fade, bleached by the sun. Traveler
Mountain is revealed, a stump of rhyolite, the hardened lava from
thousands of volcanic eruptions four hundred million years ago,

when Europe, Africa, and America were pressing against one another with incredible force. Katahdin, a much taller mountain, a black swelling of earth, hoists up the southern horizon; beyond it lies nothing. Tiny black hills cluster around the giant's sides.

Tomorrow I plan to travel on to Mount Katahdin to revisit a once-familiar landscape for the first time since childhood. Curiosity takes me there. I want to observe how much has changed in the last twenty years.

When I hike across the "summit ridge" of Katahdin tomorrow I'll be following not just my old childhood footsteps but also those of Henry David Thoreau. Perhaps the question I should be asking is: What has changed in the last century and a half? When Thoreau climbed these same hills and walked these woods only twenty million people lived in the United States; today that number tops 280 million. How much has our growing population changed the way humans interact with nature? What is it—philosophically, aesthetically, and biologically—that attracts us to nature in the first place? Can the natural world still satisfy crowds in search of solitude?

The cliché about climbing a mountain "because it's there" just won't do. I want to discover *why* it's there, geologically, and why, emotionally, I care.

So far today I've seen no one. On the summit of Black Cat a Novemberish wind brushes across the ground. Heavy and dank, the cotton in my socks sucks warmth from my toes. I sit below a stunted birch tree, its trunk a feeble windbreak, a cradle of sorts. All the trees here are short and wiry, like bushes. They have just begun to grow back after the fire of a century ago, which turned the tree-clad peaks into lumps of rock and coal.

The gusts penetrate my coat; grasses whip about; branches creak and moan. The skin of my face tightens and presses inward against the inner core of warmth. I hear a buzz behind my ear and brush at it with my hand. A mosquito flits about my scalp like an airplane negotiating the mountains. It twists and dodges, circling back. We play this game for a while, till the wind sweeps it away.

Of all the things on this windy summit only one is still: a boot-print stamped in the dirt, crisp as if left only minutes ago. The ridges in the print form a cradle of perfect size, and in this cradle, some forty miles away from the closest general store, rests a ciga-rette butt: brown, squat, dirty. It is a peel of paper wrapped around tar, a leaf blown north from the tobacco fields of the Carolinas. Protected inside its niche, the stub is motionless, while overhead, the twigs of a birch sapling rage in the wind.

Who, I wonder, scrambles up a mountain to smoke? Who is careless enough to litter on an out-of-the-way mountaintop as if it were a street corner back in town? At 2,910 feet above sea level, Black Cat is puny even in comparison to the stumps of Appalachia, but it is steep enough to paste a sticky layer of sweat to my brow— and, no doubt, to the brow of that smoker. He exerted himself to litter in this place.

Puzzled and annoyed, I pitch the stub into a pocket in my pack, where it joins an apple core and a granola bar wrapper. Should a single inch of paper and tar ruin the view? I won't allow it to.

I witness the glint of sunrise on pink Katahdin granite, while in the east, Traveler Mountain drapes shadows over South Branch Pond. From the peak, I can see Pogy Notch Trail beside a creek, winding south toward Russell Pond. Beyond lies a lowland, the pithy center of wild Maine, where the greens are softer greens, tamer than the grim bands of conifers encircling the mountains. Hardwoods thrive there, flourishing in a valley cleared by the biting saws of the logging industry, its pines and evergreens removed long ago.

Thoreau circumnavigated this land in 1857, sitting on the cross-bar of a canoe, while a stout Penobscot Indian with an oar powered the boat up the Allagash and down the East Branch. Of course, the land was not yet a park, not yet a wildlife sanctuary. Tall white pines grew on Katahdin, but Thoreau did not seek them out; he dared not climb the mountain a second time.

In 1879 a sickly, nearsighted youth named Teddy Roosevelt hiked Mount Katahdin's trails. "Speak softly and carry a walking stick," he is jokingly rumored to have said at the time. The future president of the United States was then followed by thousands upon thousands of lesser names, among them Myron Avery, the once-fiery environmentalist, and Jake Day, artist for Walt Disney, whose pictures of white-tailed deer from the mountain's foothills were once used to make the movie *Bambi*. Old names and memories are all that remain.

The sun brightens, evaporating the last of the morning fog. I gaze down at the woods and the water. Bobbing on the waves of South Branch Pond, unaware of its mortality, a loon cries.

The Appalachian Trail

In 1846 Thoreau took two full weeks to travel from Concord to Katahdin and back again. Today it's possible to drive from Boston overnight to the mountain's base, hike across the summit ridge by noon, scramble back to the parking lot in just eight or nine hours, and rush back to the city in time to cap a three-day weekend. If you hurry, you'll even have time to catch up on household chores, watch the late-night lineup on NBC, and dash off a few digital photographs and e-mails about your adventure before heading to work the next morning.

Society has sped up. We seek quick thrills—most of us. But for those who don't, there exists a longer, slower, and perhaps more rewarding route to Katahdin: the Appalachian Trail.

Slow-walking, fast-talking hikers abbreviate the name in casual conversation to "the A.T." It is a 2,160-mile footpath that begins atop Springer Mountain, Georgia, then winds, dips, climbs, and curves across the backbone of the ancient, eroded Appalachian Mountain chain all the way to northern Maine. The trail concludes at Katahdin.

My roundabout approach to Katahdin from the north, via Traveler and Black Cat Mountains, is being mirrored this summer by an estimated three thousand hikers coming from the south along the Appalachian Trail. By now they are somewhere deep in North Carolina or Virginia. They all have Mount Katahdin on their minds—and forty to sixty pounds of gear on their backs.

Those who wish for a lighter burden and a shorter journey make use of short sections of the Appalachian Trail every year, and such people are appropriately enough called "section hikers." I'll join their number tomorrow when I hike to Katahdin's summit along the last five miles of the continent-spanning trail. Section hikers number in the millions.

The rare, hardy bunch who walk the whole way to Katahdin from Georgia are called "thru-hikers." The definition invites an obvious pun. "I was just starting out in Georgia," a man named Richard Bailey once told me. "Someone asked me if I was thru-hiking. So I said, no, I still have about two thousand miles to go."

Bailey is retired. He has a graying beard, bifocals, and a humorous glint in his eye. Put a pack on his back and a walking stick in his hand and he looks a bit like Santa Claus after a shopping spree at L. L. Bean.

Back in 1987 he started hiking sections of the Appalachian Trail, inspired by an article in *National Geographic*. "I was talking to my wife about it, and she said I'd better stop talking about it and just do it. So I took three weeks off and headed to Georgia." The idea of walking the entire length of the trail all the way to Katahdin wasn't an option yet—he still was working full-time—but the thought was on his mind. "I'd worked at General Electric long enough that I had six weeks of vacation," he explained. He spent three weeks with his family and the other three on the trail. When he saved up additional vacation time, he hiked some more. By 1990 he had completed, intermittently, the full length of the Appalachian Trail.

Only one challenge remained.

In 1998 he embarked on a five-month trek from Springer Mountain to Katahdin in one start-to-finish sprint. "I had just retired, so I figured this would be a good way to do something to ease into retirement. I wanted to see how much the trail had changed in ten years."

It was early April when he started. The weather refused to cooperate, raining or snowing on twenty-three of his first twenty-eight days. "It really thinned out the hikers pretty fast," Bailey said. He was too wet to enjoy the solitude.

"Did you think about giving up?" I asked.

Bailey said no. But he met many on the trail who did. "So many people go down there with expectations," he said, "talking about Bambi and Thumper and communing with nature. They don't last long. You don't have to have a lot of hiking savvy. But if you're going out there to find yourself or find God, you're not going to do well. You've got to have a good idea of who you are before you get there."

What Bailey calls "Bambi- and Thumper-type people" seldom last beyond the very beginning of the trail. "They're not too reality based," he said. He harrumphed and rolled his eyes. "Not that thru-hikers are reality based to begin with, but a lot of people go out there to escape from the real world. Quite often they've put no thought into what they need for gear."

He encountered one ill-prepared family, a father and two sons, just north of Springer Mountain. "They were going to hike the trail but didn't have any food with them." Bailey and several other thru-hikers expressed concern. "'How you gonna live, anyway?' we asked. So the guy, who was a preacher, said, 'The Lord will provide!' They were living off lichen, that big flaky lichen that grows on rocks and has the nutritional value of newspaper. They didn't last long."

"What kind of person does last?" I asked.

"Interestingly, the typical thru-hiker doesn't look like the typical thru-hiker," Bailey said with a laugh. "I really believe the most important thing to bring on the trail is a sense of humor. If you can't laugh at yourself—and others—if you can't see humor in the fact that you got soaking wet and you don't have anyplace dry to stay and the shelter is full, if you can't see humor in that, you're not going to make it. It's not all fun and games."

One week into his months-long journey to Katahdin, Dick Bailey was already tired, wet, miserable, and unable to escape from the cold April rain. According to the best estimates, it takes five million steps to complete the Appalachian Trail; to reach Katahdin, Bailey still had about 4,865,000 steps to go.

Where the Wild Things Were

A twig nips at my face; the thorn on its tip rips out a bite of skin an inch below my eye. On my lip, there is a sudden sting of salt. I dab at the blood with a shirt sleeve. Around me, bushes sag with berries, while maples, birches, spruces, and pines all thrust their branches across my path. The air is full of wood. With two hands I try to shove open a hole big enough to step through.

A branch in my left hand tugs free and slaps at my cheek with a fist full of leaves, soggy with yesterday's rain. So, I think, this is what bushwhacking is like. Backpackers are supposed to stick to the trail, and the trail to them. But the trail is not here right now, and I am. One of us has wandered away.

A birch tree's shadow slides across the ground, a thin strip of twilight. Like an arrow, a guide, it points away from the sun, toward the mountain. I follow.

Though I see no one—no thing—I'm not alone. Watching me,

there are eyes in the shadows. Slowly I turn and stare. What sort of creature is out there? Why does it follow me?

A deer's head, antlered, furry, and brown, peeks out of a bush. I hear a tentative footstep as it kicks the grass with a hoof. We lock eyes. A second deer steps forward, a young buck. His eyes are full of distrust. Stupidly, I raise a hand in greeting.

They bound away, of course, gliding arcs of flesh and bone. Their tails bob and fly. Seconds later, they are gone.

Deer always seem to react that way to me. Years ago I encountered an entire family of deer, and they, too, vanished like a mirage.

I was riding a bicycle at dusk down a wooded road. Blacktop slid under the tires at twenty miles per hour, a blur of asphalt. Wind gusted my hair back wildly, a million short, blond flags. As the sun dipped below the hills, the sky purpled. A cornfield whisked by on my right. Tangles of maple trees barricaded the left.

Suddenly I saw them, poised along the roadside: a cluster of five deer. I slowed, stopped; the bicycle's brakes squeaked. The deer twitched their heads in unison, a snap of attention. Quickly, they bounded away. A leaf fluttered in the air, as if to fill the vacuum left in their wake.

Minutes later, back at home, I burst out excitedly to a friend, "I just saw five deer riding home on my bike!" She snorted in amusement, asking if I had shouted after them, "Hey! That's my bike!" Fortunately, deer pay scant attention to syntax and grammar.

Do wild animals always fear us when we intrude into their world? We certainly don't welcome them to ours, the world of cars and computers, strip malls and skyscrapers, pesticides and plows.

Humans are the only animals who insist, by and large, that they are not animals at all. A metaphorical wall separates us from what we call wilderness. Some of us tell nature to stick to its own side of the fence. Don't call us, we say, we'll come get you when we need you.

But nature does call. Wherever we seize and tame the land, wild nature tries to snatch it back.

Four days after a steamroller and a crew of six workers repaved the street outside my house, a grass reed poked through the tar. The road was black, hard, fresh, and yet here grew a flimsy blade of grass, as if the five inches of cement it had cut through were as soft as April mud. The grass swayed. As I stared down at it, heat rippled the air between us. I bent down and prodded the road's surface; my finger recoiled. Yet a feeble stem, a weed, had thrust through that crusty shell.

Nature ignores our metaphorical fences and walls and knocks down our real ones. In the short run, bulldozers are stronger than trees, hydroelectric dams are mightier than rivers—but can they go the distance? That question worries us.

We are born into a world of rectangular boxes, perfumed air, our nights lit by bulbs of white glass, our days quantified by the ticking circles we strap to our wrists. Other animals, like deer, sleep on pillows of maple leaves and grass. Ants dig tunnels in the soft wood of trees; bears huddle in the backs of caves. Are they really so different from us?

People are reluctant to acknowledge kinship with even the closest of our relatives, the primates. In 1860 Bishop Wilberforce of Oxford confronted the avid evolutionist Thomas Huxley. "Tell us," he sneered, "whether it is through your grandfather or your grandmother that you claim your descent from a monkey?" This occurred at a meeting of the British Association for the Advancement of Science on June 30. Huxley retaliated in defense of Darwinism, but the bishop's quip still drew a laugh.

Apes are animals, and to call them our cousins is, perhaps, to say something unpleasant about ourselves. The idea that we are God's favorite children—in fact, God's only children—dies hard. We are rude cousins at a family reunion, sulking in the corner, staring at our shoes, ashamed of our relatives. We tell the apes, the deer, the snakes, "You have your world, we have ours." The animals and the trees don't agree. At times, unexpectedly, nature will seek us out in territory we claim firmly as our own—for instance, New Jersey.

There's a barbershop on Witherspoon Street, Princeton. The floor is smooth tiled, a ceramic roof draped over a long-forgotten patch of soil. Inches below the cellar floor lies ground that has not felt a hoof, seen the sun, or fed minerals to tree roots for decades. It is a relic of wilderness, safely buried.

All that is about to change.

Outside, a deer materializes in the street. Cars honk, brakes screech. A truck backfires; the explosive echo ricochets from window to window down the street. To people on the sidewalk, this noise is like the snap of a whip's tip. They wince and cover their ears.

Startled, the doe flinches, but she does not run. There is a loud thump as the deer smacks against a car. Too late, she springs away, her hide brown and bruised, moist with blood.

Inside the shop, the two barbers and their customers know nothing of all this. New Jersey is a state of noise, car fumes, and cement—"the Traffic State." Nothing unusual occurs until a minute or two past noon, when the glass door violently explodes.

Brittle glass skips across the floor like clear, jagged hail. The doe leaps in, her eyes bloody with fear, clapping muddy hooves against the tiles.

In the seat closest to the door, a customer sucks in a nervous breath, and holds it. Hairs on the back of his neck rise through the lather. A second customer notices his mouth hung open and snaps it shut. The two barbers pause, scissors ajar.

Into a large mirror at the back of the shop, the deer throws herself; the mirror reflects the outside, and freedom. She strikes the glass with her hooves, tries to dive through, to escape in desperation like

Alice through the looking glass. Her front legs chop at the air, kicking high against the wall. Blood trickles down her fur. But always, always the image of a second deer lunges at her, pushing her back. Trapped, the doe stops at last. She turns. Splashes of blood, chips of broken glass stained red, and smears of mud lie strewn in her wake.

A man comes to his senses and runs to the broken shell of the door. He pulls it open, pressing himself close against the wall, out of the way. The deer blinks and walks away from the mirror. She peers at the man, then steps slowly through the doorway. In the street, she disappears as suddenly as she came.

The trail has found me again at last; I trudge uphill. Far ahead, the little mountain under my feet juts above the trees. The hill is a wedge of pure granite, a depository for quartz, feldspar, and black mica. There are also a number of foreign boulders called erratics, dumped here by the last continental glacier, but these intrusive chunks of rock are masked in moss, crested by a layer of thin soil.

I walk stooped; my chin droops. A rip streaks down the left side of my boot, where I sliced it against a sharp stone. I notice a ring of brown mud on my pants. The only sounds I hear are the wind in my lungs and the percussion of pebbles rattling downhill, kicked loose by my feet. The trees recede, a green blur. A sizzle of lactic acid burns across the muscles in my legs.

Pain is a distraction. That's why, perhaps, I fail to see the doe until I have practically walked into her. I look up, suddenly aware. The deer also jumps, startled. "What's her excuse?" I wonder. What could a deer possibly be doing that she doesn't notice an out-of-breath hiker huffing and puffing up the mountain?

The deer trots away two steps, three steps, then leans her head back over a shoulder. Wide, nonhuman eyes analyze me. I stare back. For a minute, then two, she watches me, head turned toward me, but body crouched, poised to flee.

I swing the pack off my back and reach quietly for my camera. Tucked under a sweater, I feel something metal and pull it out—a canteen. Good enough. I sit down on a cold slab of granite and gulp down the cool water. Water drips down my palm to my fingertips, and I flick it at the ground. The droplets smack into the mitt of a maple leaf—a satisfying sound.

The deer relaxes, lowering her head to pluck a leaf off the nearest shrub. The eyes look away for a second, then dart back. Maybe she has decided I'm harmless after all. She starts to forage on the trees and shrubs nearby. She wanders up the trail a short way, eating, ignoring me. The hiss of a distant stream echoes off the leaves. The doe clips grass.

I look and listen. Breezes are siphoned around the tree trunks. A waterfall slaps at the rocks in the distance. High in the trees, a sparrow whistles three sharp notes, then falls to silence.

The deer ignores me, as if I were a squirrel or a moose or another deer. We go about our separate business. There is a strange red stone on the ground, round and polished like a misplaced pebble of jasper; I stoop to examine it. Nearby, the doe discovers a bush of equal interest and starts to nibble. For a few minutes we share this place, the deer and I, a few steps apart.

Shadows lace the brown ground with long, dark ribbons and strings. I see the deer's white tail as a flicker, a flit of motion amid the sluggish crawl of tree shadows. Low in the west, the sun burns red on the forest floor. Rough pine bark turns dull, featureless, charred black.

It's late; I can't stay here. I rise, walking up the trail toward the deer, then past her. She glances up, not in sudden fear but in curiosity. "Where are you going," those eyes ask me. "Isn't this a nice enough place?" Her gaze follows me up the hill. When I glance back, the deer is still there, walking calmly tree to tree, leaf to leaf.

Yes, this is a nice place. But I don't live here; I am a visitor, an unexpected guest. Nonetheless I have learned that I am welcome here, to share the evening breezes and the warm tint of the setting sun. Still, in the end, I must go home.

The doe and I are kin, despite the chasm of millions of years that divides us. We are not strangers. Someday, perhaps, if I am patient enough, we will meet again.

Animal Tales

In *Ktaadn*, Thoreau evokes suspense by scurrying past several "dark and cavernous" regions on the mountain and then remarking, "These holes were bears' dens, and the bears were even then at home." But no bears chased him. Thoreau says nothing more about them, except to call the boulder-strewn region in which they live "the most treacherous and porous country I ever traveled."

Bears will invigorate any hiking story. In Bill Bryson's *A Walk in the Woods*, fear of bears remains a palpable, page-turning lure for over two hundred pages, even though the bears themselves stay conveniently offstage.

I have a bear story of my own. On what was up until that moment a peaceful autumn day, I encountered a giant bear. Alone in the deep woods of Maine, I stood face to face with five hundred snarling pounds of fur, fang, and claw. The bear towered over me, glaring down with black eyes, and I could tell there was just one thing on its mind: "lunch."

Well, not exactly. I admit that's an exaggeration. The encounter really happened five miles outside the village of Gorham, New Hampshire, close to the Maine state line. I was riding a bicycle on a side road, not walking, and I was tired; my gaze was fixed on the pavement. It's true that the bear was only a few feet away, almost close enough to touch. But before I noticed the animal, it had already turned and started to run. All I saw was its furry back vanishing into the trees. The animal had heard me coming and fled. The whole encounter lasted three seconds. End of story.

Statistics show that the familiar black bear, *Ursus americanus*, weighs eight ounces at birth, up to five hundred pounds as an adult, and commonly grows to unrealistic, elephantine proportions once a storyteller gets a hold of him.

Ever since that day, I've kept my ears open for amusing bear stories. I suspect that most of them are "improved" to some extent by the storytellers. Perhaps most, like mine, contain a grain of truth.

I learned about the bear called Brigand while sitting on the porch of a log cabin, deep in the woods of Maine. The creature didn't really deserve his nickname—Curious George would have been better—but here is how he got it.

A Baxter State Park ranger told the story. One night the ranger decided to spook his visitors—including me—in a friendly, New England sort of way. He was telling us tales about mountains, trees, the bears, and the bees.

Quickly he gathered an audience. As night fell, coyotes chortled and howled. Mount Katahdin loomed as a sky-encompassing shadow in the distance.

"Not long ago," said the red-haired ranger, "a man was hiking alone in the woods when he heard steps behind him. A bear was stalking him, loping along the trail about ten paces back." The man was scared so he walked faster. So did the bear. "No matter how fast he walked, that bear stayed just a few paces back, breathing down his neck. They went on this way for a mile or so."

Eventually the hiker panicked and broke into a run. "You guessed it, so did the bear." Of course, the man knew that he couldn't outrun a bear, so he tried to distract the beast. He tossed his jacket to the ground and then sprinted. "Sure enough," the ranger said, "that bear stopped to sniff the jacket for a second or two. And then it went right back chasing the man."

Next the man peeled off his shirt. The curious bear stopped again, sniffed the cloth. But it quickly raced after the man.

By now, the man was breathing hard, getting tired. Each time the bear caught up, the man stripped off a layer of clothing to regain his lead. Pretty soon he had no more clothes. His striptease tactics had failed.

Cold, shivering in the breeze, the man finally lay down at the edge of a pond and played possum.

"That bear loomed over him, so close he could feel its breath. With a hairy paw, it groped for his shoulder." At last, the man snapped. "He did what he should have done all along—screamed! The man yelled, leapt up, and flapped his arms wildly. Like a crazy man, he charged at the bear."

The poor bear, scared out of its wits, fled in terror and was never seen in the park again.

I don't mean to joke about the impact of bears on the wilderness experience. But for Appalachian Trail thru-hikers, on their way to Katahdin from Springer Mountain, bears have become less a true danger and more of a nuisance.

"I saw two or three bears," hiker Steve Piotrow remembers from his two-thousand-mile walk. "The only time bears were ever a concern was in the Smokies in North Carolina. The shelters were fenced in to keep them out because the bears there had become too friendly. Notorious for sneaking into the shelters and ransacking packs."

Dick Bailey shares his memories of bears in a characteristic way. "I bear-ly saw any," he puns. Getting serious, he says, "In 1998 one of the biggest changes from when I did the trail the first time and the second time, about ten years apart, was in New Jersey. They were moving problem bears into the area. So everyone going through New Jersey had a bear story." He lifts his hands in imitation of an attacking bear. "The bears were actually charging at hikers to see if they could get them to drop their packs. Bears would actually come into shelters with people there, trying to steal food."

Bailey lowers his hands and points out a section of the trail on a map. "One of the guys I hiked with showed me a picture a year later. He and I and a bunch of people stayed at this shelter in New Jersey." Bailey and most of the group packed up and left early the next morning, but two of the men stayed. They were having a late breakfast. Bailey says, "After we left, a bear came in and went right up to the edge of sleeping platform. It wanted to get up there. And the person who was there had a pole, a ski pole, and was poking at the bear to keep the bear down. He got a picture of the bear within about six feet of him."

An old reference book on my desk assures readers that black bears are "not normally vicious but never really trustworthy." Immediately following that statement is a less-than-comforting scientific analysis of bears' teeth. They have, I note, three very sharp incisors on each side of their lower jaw-bone and six more on the upper jaw.

As for food, the book describes black bears as "particularly fond of berries." But flesh, fish, fruits, and vegetables are also on the menu, including—if legends are true—the occasional unwary hiker. The noises a black bear makes are said to resemble those of any discerning restaurant critic: "a growl, a snort, and a smacking of lips."

Richard Bailey saw a bear for the first time while section-hiking in the Mahoosuc Range of Maine, south of Katahdin. "I was hiking southbound alone, and it was raining. The ambient noise level was high." In other words, he never heard the bear coming.

Bailey was crossing a log bridge. "It's kind of swampy in that area. The brush and reeds are probably about four feet high on either side. All of a sudden the brush is rustling and I see two bears climb up a tree." Meanwhile, the brush continued to rustle and sway. It took Bailey a split-second to understand what that meant. "When I saw those two bears go up the tree and I saw the brush still moving, I realized that even though they looked pretty good size they had to be cubs. What was causing the brush to rustle was mama bear. I got out of there."

During his entire two-thousand-mile journey to Katahdin along the Appalachian Trail, Bryan Yeaton of New Hampshire never once saw a bear. That lack still disappoints him. "Once I heard what I was sure were bears rustling in the woods, but I never saw them." Later that day, hikers coming along the trail behind him caught up and boasted that they had seen a mother and cubs crossing the trail. Cute, scenic, harmless. "Apparently, five minutes after I left they were leaping across the trail and everyone but me was getting pictures."

Despite the shortfall of bears, Yeaton has no regrets. Wildlife showed up all along the way. "I saw my first rattlesnake on St. Mary's Rock in Shenandoah National Park," he recalls. He moved on and was soon treated to another sight. "Twenty minutes into Shenandoah National Park I heard this rustling in the woods and thought, oh great, I'm finally going to see a bear. Then a little tufted head poked out of the underbrush and for a second we stared right at each other. It was a bobcat." His face lights up, recalling the encounter. "I was feeling pretty low, pretty tired, but that gave me a lift to carry through for the rest of the day. Something like that happened every single day."

Standing eye to eye with a bobcat—or a bear—is not an everyday experience for most of us. If we see wild animals at all they are more often problem bears raiding neighborhood garbage bins. Sometimes the culprits are wolves or coyotes, preying on housecats and farmers' livestock. Deer and moose cross our roads to their peril—and sometimes to ours.

As human industry, farmland, roads, and suburbs increasingly overlap what used to be wildlife habitat, the results range from tragic to comic to awe-inspiring. Newspaper headlines tell the tale: "Bear Sighted in Main Street Yard," "Third Black Bear Sighting Reported," "Deer Invades Barbershop."

My favorite headline is "Lost Flock of Loons Rescued by Motorists." The day was foggy, icy. Perhaps ice on their wings had forced the birds to land. Loons are aquatic creatures, not much used to stumbling about on dry land. According to an Associated Press report, the flock of loons landed on an ice-covered highway, mistaking it for a river. They couldn't walk or stand. Drivers stopped by the dozens to help rescue the loons, keeping the birds safe in cardboard boxes and warm garages until conditions improved the next day.

At times the boundary between the human and natural worlds is not clear cut. Loons get lost in fog and are forced to alter their flight plans, coyotes hunt pets and livestock, bears wander through our backyards and noisily knock over the trash cans. Wild animals continue to appear where we think they "shouldn't be."

In northern New England, moose thrive, and every year or so a bull moose wanders out of the woods and falls in love with somebody's cow.

One farmer woke up early to start morning chores, but was surprised to find a seven-hundred-pound moose wooing his pet cow, Jessica. The cow was a Hereford, a grass eater who mostly tried to ignore her new friend. The moose was a tall, awkward creature with legs like stilts and an Adam's apple the size of a grapefruit. It was a tragic case of beauty and the beast.

The young moose lingered in the area for seventy-six days, courting a cow. He quickly became a celebrity in the papers, a topic of conversation at local stores. Then alas, the romance faded. Early in January, at the end of the mating season, he lost both his antlers and his interest in Jessica.

For years I worked on a small New England farm, and each night I'd hear the yip and howl of coyotes in the hills. An old watchdog perked up her ears at the sound, ready to protect the sheep.

In the morning, I stood in an alcove of the barn, scooping pellets of feed into buckets. Sunbeams cascaded through the windows, shining an orange glow on the freshly whitewashed walls. Behind me, chickens clucked around their feeder on the floor. Outside, the sheep baaed for breakfast.

Suddenly I saw it—a flash of red in the corner of my eye. And apparently that "flash of red" saw me, too. When I turned to look, a fox spun and bolted out of the barn. Behind me, the chickens still pecked at the stone floor, unaware that a fox had almost joined them for breakfast.

I believe that most animals, like the hapless moose, have more than a quick meal on their minds. One misty autumn morning on the farm, I watched a horse and a deer touch noses over a fence line. Perhaps it was just an illusion, a mirage created by fog, distance, and my lack of sleep. Did that doe hear me coming, a clumsy, noisy human striding down the edge of the field? Had I interrupted a reunion of old friends? I'll never know. When I stepped closer, blinking in surprise, the deer was gone—vanished in the fog.

Going to Katahdin

"I have travelled widely in Concord," said Henry David Thoreau. His boast was a witty way of admitting that his books and essays cover a limited geographical range: woodlots, rivers, and hills, most of them comfortably within the borders of Massachusetts. Three trips to Maine in 1846, 1853, and 1857 mark his farthest literary excursions. Instead of traveling widely in the usual sense, Thoreau observed his local landscape in great detail. A walk in the woods around Concord or a quick hike—relatively speaking—up Katahdin became the backdrop for his thoughts, which ranged far and wide indeed.

Like Thoreau, I intend to travel widely on Katahdin today. For the first time in nearly five years I've climbed above treeline into the realm of the Native American mountain ghost Pamola, "the Cloud Maker."

I stand on the tundra of the mountain's tablelands, a field of granite thrust rudely into the sky. A herd of cumulus clouds gallops across this plain, kicking up dust. The clouds rush at me, a stampede stretching from horizon to horizon, racing a step ahead of the wind. Closer, closer they come, and here I am stuck on a mountaintop with nowhere to run. They hit, and the world explodes with whiteness.

I bend down to where the air is clear, an inch below my knees. With my hand I prod a cloud's belly; my fingers fade, swallowed by the mist.

A minute later the clouds vanish as suddenly as they appeared.

So far, no one else has set foot on the slopes to disturb my solitude. I am alone, a tiny silhouette on the ridge, with a view that stretches from here to forever.

Once the clouds pass, no shade exists above timberline. The sun burns high overhead, and even my own shadow shrinks into a tiny dark patch of ground at my feet. I stride across a boulder painted with a white blaze, marking the trail. The local guidebooks name this path the Hunt Trail, but if I follow it far enough south it will lead all the way to Springer Mountain, Georgia, over two thousand miles away. Two miles in the opposite direction will take me to the summit of Katahdin and the end of the line.

I gaze south. Beyond the horizon, hundreds of Appalachian Trail thru-hikers are pacing off the five million steps that eventually—weeks or months later—will bring them to the exact spot where I now stand.

While all trails are artificial, cut through forests at human whim, it's no accident that the Appalachian Trail ends at Katahdin. Katahdin is the highest peak of the last range of mountains on the East Coast of North America. Beyond, to the north, the mountains end. This is the brink. Walk down, and there's nowhere else from here to the horizon to walk up. The hills descend into a lowland of wide lakes and forests stretching north to Canada.

The Appalachians are done with; they are all south of here. A Spanish explorer, Hernando de Soto, named them after the Apalachee Indians, who may have pointed the way to the mountains but certainly did not live in them; they stayed in Florida and southern Georgia. But the name stuck, and was soon applied to the whole chain of mountains north of Alabama.

A few four-thousand-foot peaks rise in Quebec, far to the northeast, but they are beyond sight from the Appalachian Trail's end, invisible.* Mount Bigelow and a ridge of blue hills loom to the south, and the snowy tip of Mount Washington gleams on the New Hampshire border. Leaving the White Mountains, the trail climbs down from Mount Moosilauke into the Green Mountains of Vermont, then falls deeper into the Berkshires of Massachusetts. Winding through Connecticut, the trail crosses a narrow slice of New York and New Jersey, plunges through the hills of Pennsylvania, Maryland, and Virginia. Again, it rises out of the warmth of the southern clime to the subarctic peaks of the Great Smokies, treads along the Tennessee-North Carolina border, and rolls to a stop at

---

* In June 1999, the official opening of the International Appalachian Trail corrected this oversight. The IAT extends 520 miles across Maine and New Brunswick, and finally reaches the rugged mountains of Quebec, crossing over 4,160-foot-high Mount Jacques-Cartier, where snow lasts nearly ten months a year and caribou still roam. The trail—and the true end of the Appalachian Range—ends abruptly at the cliffs of Cap Gaspé, overlooking the Atlantic.

The new IAT was the vision of Dick Anderson, a former commissioner of Maine's Department of Conservation, who decided that a two-thousand-mile walk wasn't quite long enough. His vision is not yet complete. The "trail" through Maine is patchy so far, consisting mostly of old logging roads through privately owned land. Both paper companies and Baxter State Park (citing concerns about increased hiker traffic in an already congested area) have shown little enthusiasm for the new trail. The IAT does not cross Katahdin, instead departing from the Appalachian Trail proper at a point just south of Baxter State Park.

Springer Mountain in Georgia, the southern end of Appalachia. The last remnants of the hills trickle off into Alabama.

An estimated three thousand people set out from Springer Mountain this spring, determined to hike the entire A.T. to Katahdin. No one knows the exact number. What I do know is that most will not succeed.

"In the first week, there's probably a 10 percent dropout rate," thru-hiker Dick Bailey recalled after his own Georgia-to-Maine excursion. Hikers reach the first road crossing about three days out from Springer Mountain, and the wide, flat, paved path to the nearest town can be a temptation for hikers who already have sore feet, wet clothes, and unmet expectations. "A lot of people resupply there, and a lot of people drop out there," said Bailey. "That's the first real chance you have to rethink what you're doing."

Early on, Bailey encountered a gung ho former army ranger. "This guy kept bragging about how he was going to do thirty-mile days." The typical thru-hiker barely manages twenty. "All of us were thinking, geez, we'll never see him again. Well, that was correct. He barely made it to the top of Springer, and when I took off, I never did see him again." Bailey's eyes glinted with amusement at the memory.

"Half the people who start, it never occurs to them that they're actually going to be spending the night outdoors. It just freaks them out. There was one guy, I think he lasted about ten days. He was claustrophobic. He was staying in a tent and he just went crazy."

For Bailey, the high dropout rate was understandable. He nearly quit himself. "The third day was hell. The first day, you're running on adrenaline. It's a new experience and you meet new, strange people. Strange in a good way." After that, he said, the elation wears off. "The second day, you've started using up some of your reserves and you're starting to hurt a bit. By the third day, anyplace that could possibly hurt does."

If you can get past the that third day with no blisters, he told me, "Then you're probably going to do all right."

My friend Steve Piotrow hiked the entire Appalachian Trail in his late twenties, before (as he puts it) "becoming responsible": meeting his wife Meredith, raising a family, and embarking on a career as a science teacher. I asked him the obvious question: Why?

He had to think a moment. "Pretty much it was lack of anything better," he finally said. "I'd saved up some money, and I knew I wanted to travel, and I loved being outdoors. I like to challenge myself physically." I laughed, because that was an understatement. Steve is tall, with dark hair starting to show a hint of gray and an athleticism that has allowed him not only to hike the Appalachian Trail but also to bicycle across the continent—twice. We were talking one afternoon inside his and Meredith's log cabin in Jackson, New Hampshire, about a half hour's drive from where the Appalachian Trail descends Mount Washington and veers into Maine.

As we spoke, Steve held his five-month-old son, Foster. I sat at the kitchen table. Steve explained that the simplicity of the trail appealed to him in much the same way that the simplicity of living in a cabin at Walden Pond appealed to Thoreau. "The A.T. was two thousand miles and about three months of traveling where I wouldn't have to worry about anything but where I was going to sleep and what was I going to eat," he said.

Just then the baby began to cry. Steve stood and paced around the room with the baby in his arms until Foster quieted; the movement had a soothing effect. Apparently just sitting still is not something that runs in the family.

Steve started his trip alone, riding a train to Georgia and hopping on a bus to Savannah. "From there I started hoofing it. I wanted to break in my feet a little bit by the time I reached the trailhead. I think I actually broke them in too well at the beginning, because I was just hiking on paved roads about fifteen miles a day. My feet were sore."

His first day out from Springer Mountain was lonely. "I didn't see anybody, but I knew there were a lot of people in front of me because I'd gotten a late start." It was late April, and most thru-hikers had started weeks earlier in order to beat the early onset of winter on Katahdin.* Steve hustled to catch up. On the third day, at one of the hostels along the trail, he ran into "Bubba."

Bubba was an ex-navy seal. "He and I got to be kindred spirits right off the bat," Steve said. "We were both trying to do a lot of miles. We were out there for the same reasons, just to be out there. We teamed up for a month and a half."

Bubba was not Steve's only companion during the long walk to Katahdin. "I really thought I was going to be out there on my own, having to depend on my own resources. But after five days of being alone, I thought it would be kind of nice to see someone else."

Thoreau went to Katahdin with a plan and a companion—his cousin George Thatcher—during his famous two-week expedition in 1846. In 1998 Dick Bailey set out alone. "I couldn't find anyone else to go with me. Let's face it, it takes a certain kind of strange individual to be doing this in the first place."

He was not alone for long. On the very first day he encountered others, all with the common goal of walking to Katahdin.

Surprisingly, Bailey observed that most people who started the Appalachian Trail together in Georgia didn't arrive together at Katahdin. "Generally, it doesn't work out well. The people who go together, unless they're a married couple, don't finish together." He

---

* Hiking the Appalachian Trail from south to north really is a race against the seasons. Though Katahdin offers a visually dramatic end point to the trail, a minority of thru-hikers chooses to travel from north to south instead, allowing a later start. That way there is less urgency, less need to keep pace with the changing seasons. Winter arrives early in northern Maine, and earlier still on the slopes of Katahdin. Baxter State Park officials close the park on October 15, or when the weather turns wintry.

explained: "You gravitate toward people who are hiking about the same speed you are and have about the same sense of humor."

My friend Steve concurred. A fast walker, he steadily overtook the hikers who had gotten an early start. But sometimes he slowed his pace, just for company. "I wouldn't say it was crowded, but I definitely wouldn't call it solitude either," he remembered. "There's definitely an A.T. community. You might run into the same people every day depending on how many miles you're hiking and what shelters you're staying at. You're pretty likely to see some people over and over again. After a while, maybe because you crave the company a little bit, you kind of slow down or speed up so you can stay with other people. I think a lot of the reason people do it is for that community feeling. You belong."

The community feeling can be overwhelming for those who take to the woods expecting privacy. One of my co-workers, Bryan Yeaton, believes that the culture along the Appalachian Trail has changed since the 1980s, when he completed his first thru-hike. "Many, many more people are hiking the trail in its entirety," he says. "When I did it, about four hundred people started and maybe ninety finished. Nowadays it's usually between three or four thousand starting and around four hundred finishing."

In 1986 Yeaton set out from Springer Mountain with two friends whom he had met doing trail work for the Appalachian Mountain Club. "We all finished—separately. Everyone has different paces and likes and dislikes."

Yeaton, a youthful forty, is still an avid hiker and outdoorsman. He section-hikes the A.T. when he can. "A lot of the solitude is gone," he says. "So I'm glad I did it when I did. But I would certainly do it again in a heartbeat. There are other trails out there, too. There's the Pacific Crest National Scenic Trail and the Continental Divide Trail. So maybe there are other worlds to explore."

His comments make me wonder: Are we obsessed with solitude? I've heard that our aloofness sometimes startles Europeans, whose continent has a greater population density and whose footpaths seldom stray far from towns and villages. In the United States we adopt an all-or-nothing approach to wilderness. Not much middle ground exists between a desire for raw, untamed forest in one place and strip malls and asphalt parking lots in another. Perhaps our growing population eventually will force that attitude to change.

What bothered Yeaton more than the presence of other people on the trail was "the way some of them behaved. Making a lot of noise, washing dishes in the streams and the water sources." He completed his trek in what he calls "the pre-crowd days." He explains: "Even though you're hiking with a couple other folks and you meet other people, most of that happens at night. During the day you're on your own. So I had plenty of solitude on the trail. I don't know if you can get that now. Maybe I'll see some day."

"The A.T. is different from the Pacific Crest Trail," according to Dick Bailey. "It's more of a social event. It's like a roving party. One guy I hiked with termed it 'the world's longest, thinnest community.'"

Bryan Yeaton likens the trail to "a big transient family."

Says Bailey, "The biggest appeal is not the sky or the fact that there are some great views out there, but the people you meet along the way. You find after a while that there's a group of people hiking about the same speed you are. You've all gone through the same nasty weather, so you have somewhat of a common bond."

The most unique social aspect of hiking the long way to Katahdin is the adoption of trail names. The name on his birth certificate was not the same one Bailey jotted down on hostel and camp registers. For five months, from Springer to Katahdin, he was known by the moniker "Old Phart."

He once met an Englishman nicknamed Sunburn. "In England they don't have much sun," Bailey explains. "He got that name because he quickly sunburned. Most people start the A.T. around the first of April, give or take two weeks, and the leaves aren't out on the trees yet. So if it is a sunny day, you've got to worry about sunburn."

After a few weeks on the trail, Bailey met a man nicknamed Sunray. "He and his father had planned to do the trail together. His father died of cancer, so he was the son, Ray, who was now hiking the trail." There also was a man called Hundred Pound Stormcloud. "This guy started out with a hundred pounds of gear and very quickly jettisoned the cans of beans and cast-iron frying pans." Bailey laughs.

Late in the spring, when Bailey reached the eastern half of the Smokies, from Icewater Springs to Davenport Gap, he endured two solid days of snow. "It stayed just below freezing all that time. I was just warm enough for the snow to melt when it hit me."

His clothes were soaked, and to fend off hypothermia he had to keep walking. "I once went twelve point five miles without taking any break. I had Raman noodles shoved inside the top of my coat, which I was eating." He dared not stop to fix a more elaborate meal. Stopping even for a moment caused shivering.

The days were endless. All he could do was put one foot in front of the other and hope eventually to walk into tomorrow.

Such cold, stormy weather is a common theme in thru-hikers' recollections. "The coldest I've ever been in my life actually turned into one of my favorite stories, one of the best things that's ever happened to me," says Bryan Yeaton. He and a friend had just climbed Dragon's Tooth, a rock spire in southern Virginia. The temperature was close to fifty degrees, not unusually cold, "but the rain was blowing horizontally. We just got absolutely soaked."

Coming down off Dragon's Tooth, Yeaton started trembling. He was dangerously hypothermic. "You know what wind and water and temperature can do." He and his friend, Lake, found a little store near where they planned to camp. "When we stopped, my body chilled down even more. I was shaking so violently I couldn't work the zippers on my pack. Lake was trying to set up the tent and wasn't doing too well."

Hypothermia is a dangerous drop in the body's core temperature, resulting in shivering, slurred speech, and disorientation. Left on their own in such a condition, Yeaton and Lake could have died. But help came from an unexpected source.

"This good ol' boy, all decked out in camo gets out of his Jeep. He takes a look at me and says, 'What are you doing, boy?' I said, 'Hiking . . . *sir*.' He goes, 'You're crazy!' and I just said, 'Yes sir.'" Bryan laughs, describing how the man walked into the store, then came back out and cast another incredulous glance at the freezing hikers. "Boy, you're crazy," the man said again. "Get over here!"

Yeaton walked over and was handed a flask. Bourbon. He drank. "I figured it was not the time to tell him that this would actually make me more hypothermic by draining the heat out of my body core," he says. "I took a hit and started to feel it tingle and started to warm up."

They talked for a while. "He was a Vietnam veteran," says Yeaton. "He told me about the coldest he'd ever been in his life, when it was very warm outside, during the monsoon rain season." The veteran offered them a place to stay—with a roof. "We went over to a cabin that he was building in the woods with another Vietnam vet. Both of them had pretty significant post-traumatic stress. We stayed with them a couple days, drying out our stuff, swapping stories, doing a little work around the cabin."

The first night, the two veterans left to go to a group counseling session. "They left these two Yankee boys in charge of their cabin," says Yeaton. "Of course, it was in the middle of nowhere, so we couldn't have found our way out anyway. The second night they came back. My friend Lake and this guy Ron both played guitar, so we sat around doing a little music. They started talking, telling us what it was like being foot soldiers on the ground in Vietnam." He pauses, takes a breath. "That was probably *the* most potent educational experience in my life. I learned an incredible amount, some very scary stuff." Then it was time to get back to the trail, to continue onward to Katahdin.

There was a parting gift. "Ron cut me this hiking stick made out of hickory, and I carried it the rest of the way," says Yeaton.

"I still have it to this day. My trail name—everyone on the trail has a nickname—was Queequeg the Harpooner because I was an English-teacher wannabe at the time, and *Moby Dick* was absolutely my favorite book. The hiking stick became my harpoon. I'm going to be buried with that stick."

Hikers along the Appalachian Trail pass by countless small towns during their five-month walk in the woods. Road crossings are frequent, and for a thru-hiker who craves company—or a restaurant dinner or hot shower—a detour to the nearest village is always welcome. "You're all clean, maybe for the first time in ten days," Bryan Yeaton says. "When you get used to the amenities, it's hard to leave it. The worst part is you've got a full pack again. Too much weight. And it seems like even if you take a day off, it takes a couple days for your legs to get back into shape. But then once you're out there you get into a rhythm and soon the town's just a distant memory."

Sometimes hikers have trouble getting back on the trail. "It's like being sucked into a black hole," says Dick Bailey. "They go into town and just never come out. People who take long breaks start getting farther and farther behind the people they'd been hiking with. That gets a little demoralizing. A lot of people who spend too much time in towns drop out for that reason."

A symbiosis exists between towns close to the trail and the hikers who pass through. "A lot of the towns make a lot of their money off hikers," says Bailey. The hikers are outsiders, and yet the local economy depends on hikers' business. "If I was going into a town for supplies I would generally buy food there because that would help the people there."

By and large, the people he met in town were friendly, especially in the south. "A guy in one of the stores down there—a gas station and little variety store—said 'You haven't been here for a couple of years, have you?' He remembered seeing me from a couple years earlier!"

That type of gregariousness lessened once he reached the northern end of the trail. "It's not that the people here are less friendly," says Bailey. "It's just that generally in New England it takes a couple generations to warm up to you."

The camaraderie along the trail is shared at times by kindhearted people in nearby towns. "Thru-hikers like people who drop in and give them beer, soda, junk food," Bailey says. "Anything rich in carbohydrates. It's like going to the zoo and feeding animals. We're very appreciative—but don't get your hand too close!" He laughs. "That's trail magic. The people who do that are called trail angels."

Trail magic is the hiking equivalent of karma. If you give food to strangers, you'll get food from strangers. "It's an important part of the trail, says Bailey. He recalls section-hiking the A.T. in Pennsylvania during a drought year. "People going through Pennsylvania would find plastic gallon jugs of water at road crossings so they wouldn't run out of water."

Bailey's favorite example of trail magic involves a blind man named Bill Irwin and his three-year-old German shepherd, Orient. Together Irwin and Orient hiked the entire Appalachian Trail in 1990, to much media fanfare. Orient, a trained seeing-eye dog, served as navigator. Their trail name was "the Orient Express."

Dick Bailey was doing his own share of trail magic that year. Just west of New Hampshire's Mount Moosilauke he dropped off food and drink at a shelter called Jeffers Brook. "Jeffers Brook is an easy shelter to walk into," he says. "It's a five-minute walk if you're slow. So I'd go in there with beer and Pepsi and food occasionally, and see who was going through."

One day he met Bill Irwin and Orient there. "Bill figures he fell down about five thousand times doing the A.T.," says Bailey. "So I stopped there at Jeffers Brook and gave him some trail magic. Bill is a minister, a born-again Christian, and a reformed alcoholic, but he's not pushy about it. He's a good person to know."

Bailey found out how true that was in 1998, while doing his own thru-hike. "Bill Irwin had moved up to Sebec, Maine," says

Bailey. "As I was going through the Hundred Mile Wilderness, just before I entered the campsite, Bill had a food kitchen set up on the trail. He was feeding anyone who came through the trail a spaghetti dinner. Dessert and everything." Both men had memories of their meeting eight years earlier. "I reminded Bill he was actually paying me back, because it was me who had given him some trail magic in 1990. I also misquoted the Bible to him, which he got a chuckle out of. It was 'Be not forgetful to entertain strangers, for by doing so many have entertained trail angels.' Bill thought that was funny."

Trail magic has sustained many a weary hiker. "A lot of people who have been on the trail have had people give them something. Obviously you can't give it back to that same person, so the best way is to pass it on to someone else."

The first glimpse of Katahdin is a momentous one. It's worth a pause, a gathering of thoughts. What the mountain hikers have been imagining for over two thousand miles is suddenly a reality. That means that the familiar, daily routine they have known is soon to change.

Steve Piotrow spotted the mountain at a distance of dozens of miles away, at a time when he was almost ready to quit. "I was definitely sick of it by the end. It's probably politically incorrect to say that. I wasn't really enjoying it. I wasn't really remembering anything I had seen."

He forced himself to go on, in a daze. "I was just hiking, head down, to get it over with. It's my own fault probably for hiking too hard." He describes "twelve days of soggy feet" and steady downpours in Maine. Mosquitoes attacked him. Those are his most vivid memories of the Hundred Mile Wilderness.

The sun appeared on the last day, as step by step he walked the last five miles to the summit of Katahdin. Then it was over, time to start a new chapter in his life.

"It was an easy transition for me because I was meeting some friends in Millinocket the day that I came down from Katahdin," says Steve. "We were driving up to Ontario for a weeklong white-water canoe trip. After that I eased back into civilization again. I had a job starting two weeks after that, teaching at a school in Delaware. So I really didn't have any time to think about how I wished I was back in the woods."

In 1998 Richard Bailey first saw Katahdin from thirty miles out, near Whitecap Mountain. "Whitecap has an excellent view of it. By the time they get there, some people get a little contemplative and are wondering whether they should slow down and make the experience last. For some people it's the biggest thing that's ever happened to them in their whole life, ever. So they don't want to hurry the end."

Bailey puts himself in the opposite camp. He was eager to be done. "Still, it's interesting to see Katahdin for the first time and realize that that's actually the goal, the holy grail you've been trying to find for almost six months. It's not just a concept anymore." Two more days of walking brought him to the boundary of Baxter State Park and the campground at Daicey Pond. "With most people, that's where it really hits them big time, about ten-and-a-half miles from Katahdin.

"When you actually get to Baxter Peak, you see the thing that looks like a sandwich board," he says, referring to a large wooden sign on the summit. "A lot of people go up and kiss it. But I said, 'Is that all there is?'" He laughs. "There's a lot of different responses. One guy who finished when I did it in '98, he just sat there. He wasn't sure what to do next."

Others had stranger reactions. "It's like post-traumatic stress," says Bailey. "They get home and they can't sleep in beds, so a lot of them sleep on the floor for a few weeks. Or in the backyard in a tent." He snorts. "I just wanted a beer and a pizza. But some people, it takes them probably six months to fully readjust to getting back to society." Some never get over the experience. "People do go out and hike year after year. Or instead of going back to school or whatever job they had, they'll work in a ski area—or maybe on the top of Mount Washington."

Bryan Yeaton—currently an employee of the Mount Washington Observatory—remembers his own response to his first glimpse of Katahdin. He said aloud, "Boy, that's still a long way away."

His emotions were mixed. "There were times every single day when I wanted to stop, and there were times every single day when I never wanted to be anyplace else. The latter feelings were the more overpowering." When he reached the summit, all he could think to do was stand by the summit and have his picture taken. "The day that I summited was a pretty decent day, and people I had met along the way were there. Probably eight or ten of them—folks I had known from earlier points on the trail. So it was kind of fun."

Adapting to the change was, perhaps, more difficult than the two-thousand-mile hike itself. "You're used to burning maybe between six thousand and ten thousand calories a day. And when you get off the trail, no matter how much running and biking you do, you gain weight. And there's a huge psychological adjustment. I had to take a job quickly to start to pay off some bills. So I worked as a retail manager for a year. It was the most awful year of my life. After that, every job I've done has involved the backcountry in some way. You can't get it out of your system."

He grins. "I thought it was going to be a great hike, a great challenge, but it turned out to be so much more than that," he says. "Even the times when I was cold and miserable and wet—in retrospect those are great war stories. You can look at a map of the trail and put your finger on any point and say *oh yeah* and remember the adventure from that day. Every day was an adventure."

Yeaton sums up the experience this way: "A lot of people go out there to find themselves, and I didn't really. But it certainly ended up changing the focus of where my life was heading. It gives you confidence. If you can accomplish something like that, you can say, 'Hey, I can do anything I want.'"

Baxter Peak

In 1927 a surveyor named Floyd Neary lugged a packful of spirit levels and other equipment up a steep, boulder-strewn shoulder of Mount Katahdin as part of a topographical study for the United States Geological Survey. On the highest peak, knee-deep in clouds, he drilled a hole in a rock and plugged it with a U.S.G.S. benchmark, listing the mountain's elevation. That benchmark, a brass plate stapled to a boulder, recorded one regrettable fact: Katahdin, the tallest mountain in Maine, stood just short of a mile above the sea. It was an accurate estimate, but disappointing; earlier surveyors had judged Katahdin safely over the mile mark. To remedy this imperfection, a cairn of rocks thirteen feet high was built at the summit, Baxter Peak. It is now possible in the state of Maine to climb a mountain and touch a small stone exactly 5,280 feet above sea level.

This is not a spectacular height. Hikers who leave Roaring Brook at sunrise can climb above timberline by late morning, trek across the four tallest of Katahdin's peaks before sunset, and still scramble back to the parking lot in time for a late dinner in Millinocket. Katahdin is dwarfed by the Rockies and the Sierras. Even in the east, several of the White Mountains of New Hampshire tower over the mountain by hundreds of feet. Katahdin suffers, like all eastern mountains, from old age. Ice splits boulders, rivers cut through bedrock. Steep peaks that once cast a shadow across New England settle into the gentle, tree-topped hills of today.

Age and erosion have not completely robbed the mountains of splendor. The heights still offer breathtaking views, and the panorama of woods and lakes attracts the interest of artists, photographers, and nature lovers.

A feeling for this land drew one individual to dedicate his life to its preservation—his gift to the people of Maine. His name was Percival P. Baxter, governor of Maine from 1921 to 1925. Though Baxter's upbringing and personality were polar opposites of Sierra Club founding-father John Muir's, both men had an impact on the environmental scene in the early twentieth century. Though they never met, passion and persistence drove them both to achieve the impossible.

Muir, a man who once danced through the night in the midst of a mountain blizzard to keep from freezing to death, later threw his full weight with equal passion into the struggle to protect the mountains of California. He enlisted Teddy Roosevelt in his cause but wept with failure near the end of his life when a dam flooded Yosemite's twin valley, which he loved. Percival Baxter, too, fell in love with a mountain and devoted much of his life to trumpeting its cause. Baxter saw no need to proselytize about the environment. His unique brand of environmentalism bypassed some of the more radical techniques now in favor: angry confrontations, spiking trees, letter writing, and referendums. He soon lost patience with political lobbying. Instead, he took the genteel approach. Baxter's tools were good manners and a wallet full of cash.

In 1882 Baxter hiked the woods and hills with his father, learning respect for the forest and the mountains, and earning in the process the unusually large sum of ten dollars per pound for every fish he caught. When he caught an eight-pounder, his father, to teach his son the value of money, put eighty dollars in the bank under Percival Baxter's name. He was six years old.

As an adult, Baxter looked like a typical New England patriarch — tall, blond, the son of a wealthy businessman — but he didn't always fit the role. Year after year he lobbied for the establishment of a state park but met with hostility from the government and apathy from the voting public. A proud Republican, he was branded a socialist, a traitor to his class.

"Shall any great timberland or paper-making corporation, or group of such corporations, themselves the owners of millions of acres of Maine forests, say to the People of this State, 'You shall not have Mount Katahdin?'" Baxter pleaded in 1921, shortly after taking office as president of the state senate.

A week later, Governor Frederic Parkhurst took ill and died, and Baxter unexpectedly succeeded him as governor of Maine. But his words still had no effect. By the end of his second term as governor, Baxter had at last lost all patience. "Those who opposed me no doubt felt relieved when I retired from the governorship to private life," he said. "But oftimes defeats can turn into victories." With the fortune he had inherited from his father, Baxter bought the land himself and deeded it to the state — on condition that it remain forever wild, unique among America's parklands.

He may not get his wish. Today, decades after Baxter's death, small mill towns and farm communities slowly die, suffocated by a sudden shift in the economic winds. Meanwhile, millions upon millions of recreation-hungry travelers race to the resorts, parks, and beaches of Maine in the first month of summer. They inject the local economy with a dose of money and then leave it to hibernate on its profits until the next tourist season. Governor Baxter saw them coming: the cars, the crowds, the noise.

Baxter remembered a time when the timber industry owned the land, pumping logs to Bangor and other cities the old-fashioned way, down the watery veins of the Penobscot River, instead of hauling them in trucks and trains. But all this was changing, and swiftly.

"Progress in the electrical world is bewildering," Baxter told the state legislature in the first month of 1924. "Electrical energy, power, is the foundation of modern civilization and people today cannot imagine to what extent 'power' will enter into the everyday life of the citizen a generation hence." This prediction was not his only instance of foresight. In one letter, he expressed his fear of the "encroachment" of jazz in the pure air—among other things, radio waves could only be tuned out, not kept out. What would he think of today's rock 'n' roll tourists, bumper-to-bumper traffic, cable TV, cell phones, the Internet, and the incessant blare of honking horns?

At the turn of the twentieth century, towns quickly moved north at the heels of the paper companies. Places uninhabited by humans in 1882 today boast shopping malls and condominiums, an expansion financed largely by cutting trees, making paper, and selling tourism. Baxter foresaw a danger to the natural heritage he loved and prepared to meet it. He bought the land himself, acre by acre for over thirty years. The result was a 202,064-acre wilderness park, terminus of the Appalachian Trail.*

Baxter was adamant on one point: nature comes before recreation, always and forever. Roads invited an intrusion of cars, noise, gas, and litter. He opposed them. Snowmobiles and the reckless freedom they allowed were considered a special curse. A photograph of a snowmobile driven miraculously to the summit in 1965

---

* Recent land acquisitions have increased Baxter State Park's size to 204,733 acres or roughly 375 square miles.

horrified the elderly Mr. Baxter, and he begged the park supervisor to ban the machines completely.

Behind his gift lay a purpose that went well beyond a wish to protect the environment or a personal need to be remembered as a great man. As a boy he had roamed the woods and streams, fished in the Penobscot with his father. He had seen the giant white pines before they tumbled and fell, and the last caribou before they were hunted to extinction. "I have talked with woodsmen who distinctly remember these strange animals as they grazed over this elevated feeding ground, or stood on the edge of the mountain looking over into the great space beyond."

A feeling for the woods stayed with him. "A boy or girl who is kind to animals and birds," he said, "learns also to be kind to boys and girls."

Baxter loved all animals, but he loved his park more. In a visit to the park in 1961, the former governor noticed the absence of squirrels and rabbits, and deer and moose as well, that had once come to picnic grounds without fear. He asked why, and was told that the tourists' dogs had chased them all away. From that moment forward, all pets were banned within park limits—a difficult decision for a man who, while in office, had once ordered the flags at the Capitol lowered to half-mast after the death of his Irish setter, Garry. Following the ban on pets came a ban on trailers and trucks. Trail bikes were stopped at the gates. Radios were forbidden.

"I do not intend that the Park forever shall be a region unvisited and neglected by man." But, he added in the same breath, "I seek to provide against commercial exploitation, against hunting, trapping and killing, against lumbering, hotels, advertising, hot-dog stands, motor vehicles, horse-drawn vehicles and other vehicles, air-craft, and the trappings of unpleasant civilization."

In other words, don't simply come to the woods. *Come simply.*

The Cloud Maker

Mountains have always failed to draw the great crowds of people that storm our beaches and ballparks every blue-skied summer day. Too much work is involved—too much dirt, sweat, and rock. Even Thoreau "slumped, scrambled, rolled, bounced, and walked, by turns, over this scraggy country" to a high ridge in the clouds, only to turn back cold, scared, and impressed. "I arrived upon a side-hill," he wrote, "where rocks, gray, silent rocks, were the flocks and herds that pastured, chewing a rocky cud at sunset. They looked at me with hard gray eyes, without a bleat or a low. This brought me to the skirt of a cloud, and bounded my walk that night."

A special horizon exists on mountaintops, a view like nowhere else on Earth. Is this enough to draw us here? The world radiates out in a perfect circle, deep and distant in all directions, with no higher hills to block the view, no trees to get in the way. I stand on a mound of rock near the summit, turning slowly to the four cardinal directions. Below, above, in all directions, lies endless space, bounded only by haze where the curve of the earth sinks below the horizon. The world is a panorama of stark colors—green forests, blue lakes, shelves of pink granite on the upper slopes.

Clouds rumble overhead, driven by the wind. I look up, then down into the woods, and see two separate beings: a cloud and a shadow. The shadows of clouds are not clipped to the heels of their twins like those of earthbound creatures. Cloud shadows do strange things; they assert their freedom, make use of their independence. In a crowded sky it's all but impossible to find a shadow's twin. You may think you see it—there, a cloud shaped just right—but then the cloud lurches forward and the shadow refuses to follow.

On the ground, those dark fluid creatures are their own animal. Even now, a small shadow—a mile long—is rooted in a groove between two rock-topped hills. The wind is fierce, northwesterly, herding the clouds toward the distant sea. But the shadow has no substance, no mass; it doesn't feel the wind. It just sits there, resting on the flanks of two hills while the clouds race by. Eventually the shadow stirs, scrambling over a hill as if in a hurry to catch up with its cloud. Then it turns and runs through the trough of a valley, sliding out of the woods toward the Atlantic Ocean.

It's a curious experience, watching the back end of a shadow rush forward. For a while the land is darkened by a wide patch of twilight spreading across miles of trees, with bright sunlight aglow at its fringes. A line between dark and light glides over hills. The line seems slow and steady, but in seconds it mounts a hill a human would take hours to climb on foot. The line flies closer, closer; behind it rushes bright sun. When it hits, the world is lit with the suddenness of a pulse of electricity, a flick of a switch.

I walk forward toward a hiker burdened with a heavy pack, who is sitting on a ledge three-quarters of a mile from Pamola Peak. He dangles his feet over the ledge. One step down lies Chimney Pond, a brown puddle lost in fog nearly two thousand feet below. This seems a strange and dangerous place for a rest, but the man just sits there. He breathes in the fresh air and absorbs the landscape with his eyes. His teeth crunch down loudly on an apple, and wind ripples the nylon fabric of his jacket. The brown pack on his back looks expensive, weighted down with a sleeping bag and a folded tent. The outer shell of the pack is a mesh of flaps and pockets, stitched loosely together like the bellies of a hundred kangaroos. It seems a wonder he can carry it all, though he is a large man, his chin clothed in a thick, reddish beard. Aluminum cups protrude from one pocket in his pack, and his feet, swaying contentedly back and forth over a cavity of open space, are wrapped in two-hundred-dollar hiking boots. This is no tourist for a day. He means to go somewhere, far away—perhaps the journey involves five million footsteps down the Appalachian Trail.

I don't expect him to speak, but he does. "You never get anywhere once you're up here because you keep stopping to admire the view." A hint of a smile appears on his face. Is this an apology? The trail is only a few feet wide, and he is perched in its middle. I have to wait for him to shift to one side, and behind me stands a family of four.

It's crowded today on the mountain. People are climbing down off the last leg of the Appalachian Trail, or else taking this steep route to the summit, Baxter Peak, from there to descend into the Great Basin to spend the night in a lean-to at Chimney Pond. The wind lashes the scraggly rocks above treeline, wonderfully fierce. It is like a savage child, eager to toss and whirl, but it finds nothing suitable to play with. The last trees stand two miles back, contorted as if in pain, bent into odd shapes by the harsh climate. A row of these dwarf trees circles the mountain, drilling thick roots into the rocks to find nourishment. Once the trees are left behind, the wind finds only boulders, which it cannot stir. It must satisfy itself with stray hikers, or mosquitoes and birds flung up from below.

A woman walks by, nods to the man. A gust flings her tress of black curls over one shoulder, pointing the way to Baxter Peak. She shivers and grins. "God! I don't like wind!" Her face, though, is delighted, flushed red with cold and with pride at having made it so far. It's a delightful scare to stand on a narrow ledge and be pushed toward death by an arctic wind. But the wind is on our side today, blowing us toward the ledge rather than off it.

In 1837 a man named William Larrabee was standing not far from here when he slipped on the icy rocks and dislocated his shoulder. Forced to spend a night in a howling September blizzard, the experience tainted his point of view. Larrabee was a writer, given to exaggerating details, and the pain of his shoulder did not help matters—nor did the lack of fire and food. To his eyes, a body that stumbled off the Knife Edge's jagged crags would see a flash of blurred granite and then plummet like a missile onto the shores of Chimney Pond, thousands of feet below. Of the wind he wrote, "One of the company, with comic gravity, inquired how many men it might take to hold one's hair on."

Larrabee was a part of a scientific expedition led by the Massachusetts state geologist, Charles Jackson. Jackson and his ten-man crew had left Bangor on the thirteenth of September in a pair of bateaux. They followed the West Branch of the Penobscot upriver to Katahdin, guided by an Indian named Louis Neptune.

In Old Town, Jackson had asked the Indians if he would find many rocks on the mountain. The reply was "Ah! Too many!"

Jackson's reasons for climbing Katahdin were political. Though the stated goal of the expedition was a general geological survey of Maine, it was also designed to bolster the American side of a dispute over the boundary between United States and British Canada— and avert a war. Katahdin, because it was the tallest point of land in the state, was a favorite site for surveyors from both sides of the issue to prove their case. From the summit it was possible to see, or claim to see, landmarks hundreds of miles away and to calculate the distances between them.

In a letter to the governor, Jackson wrote, "I was especially anxious to record the marked topographical features of a country that would necessarily become the theatre of action in case of war. . . . The claim set up by Great Britain to more than ten thousand square miles of the territory of Maine is certainly too absurd for serious refutation."

Katahdin's white peaks greeted Jackson with plumes of snow. Food ran short and was rationed, and Jackson carefully paced his assistants. Climbing over boulders and sharp rocks slick with ice, they at last arrived at the summit. But thick mists, strong winds, and a September blizzard struck hard, forcing some of the party to turn back. Louis Neptune saved their lives by building small cairns on the tablelands, markers that guided them back to a rock slide above their camp, sheltered in the trees.

Jackson called the weather bad luck. His Indian guide disagreed. "I expected this," he scolded Jackson. "This is the vengeance of Pamola on those who dare presume to measure the height of the mountain." Jackson measured it anyway. His estimate was 5,300 feet—just over a mile, but a satisfying result nonetheless. Jackson's calculations and topographical survey helped avert a full-scale war over the disputed lands. At long last the people of Maine knew which flag to fly on the Fourth of July.

Pamola was a god, and Katahdin was his home. He did not suffer trespassers on the "Greatest Mountain."

Human religion and mythology almost always place the gods on the highest possible pinnacle. Zeus and his immortal cohorts gazed upon the world from the vantage point of Mount Olympus, far above the clouds. Moses climbed into the rarefied air of a lofty peak to receive the stone tablets upon which his god's commandments were carved.

According to the Abenaki Indians of Maine, the barren, cloudy timberline of a mountain such as Katahdin was sacred ground, a meeting place for the gods. "Do not go where men stand taller than the trees," a proverb warned. Few listened; many paid with their lives. On other mountains, on Denali and Everest—on summits large and small—the story and the taboo is much the same.

One Abenaki legend tells that the spirits of nature once held their yearly conferences in the woods but were unhappy because humans sneaked behind tree trunks to spy on them, or else disturbed them with noise and chatter in the distance. They needed a place where the animals of the woods and the Indians could not or would not go. The spirits gathered in council and soon agreed that the solution was to build a mountain. Whereupon a pillar of solid rock rose out of the ground with a thunderous noise, spilling boulders across the landscape, until it towered over the older hills. Now, between mortals and the gods lay a mysterious layer of clouds. The gods could confer on the tablelands—long alpine meadows strewn with broken rocks and scrub growth—and the secrets of nature would be safe. They decreed, "No mortal shall ever climb this mountain beyond where the trees and bushes grow."

One of the Abenaki spirits, *Bahmolai*—called Pamola by less agile tongues—has always delighted storytellers and historians. In many retellings of Indian folklore he appears as the sole god of the alpine tundra. The other Abenaki spirits get passing mention, but the best stories are about Pamola. Perhaps this is because he is a nature god and a trickster, and thus fascinated the members of a Christian culture. A Catholic missionary translated Pamola's name as "He Curses on the Mountain," and branded him a demon.

Pamola was snubbed by the gods and never invited to their meetings on the tablelands, for he was ugly, encumbered with a head the size of four horses and a beak for a nose. Wild with anger, he screamed gusty daggers of words, cursing his fellow gods. His tantrum stirred the winds.

"Let him rage," sighed the gods, "For what are his words but loose air."

Kabeyun, god of the West Wind, soothed the tempest stirred

up by Pamola. When all was settled and quiet once again, the gods continued their council. Pamola paced resentfully in the shadows just beyond their campfire. His talons raked at the granite slopes. In a final fit of rage, he cleaved open a great gash in the stone; it split the mountain ridge between two jagged peaks, and the gap was as prominent and ugly as a missing tooth. This, the gods noticed. Pamola was thereafter confined to that cleft in the rocks whenever the gods met, and it bore his name.

Pamola lived a lonely life. His home was a cave set high in a granite wall. Deep in the cave Pamola slept on a bed of ice and a pillow of snow, safe from the heat of July. From the cave he gazed down at the mountain he considered his own. He was well above treeline, with a clear view into the woods below, speckled with glacial ponds. It was easy to spot intruders. Whenever people tried to climb to Pamola's cave, he hurled boulders at them, setting avalanches of rock in motion until the intruders were dead, their bones crushed, or else driven away in terror. If, by some chance, the visitors succeeded in climbing above treeline while Pamola slept, he would shout curses, filling the air with noise and wind, rain and snow. When a winter wind shrieked through the cracks of the Knife Edge, five thousand feet straight up, Abenaki hunters in the northern woods believed it was Pamola howling his anger at gods and men.

Folklore is the way a religion dies; pious tales of myth and morality dissolve centuries later into laughter around a campfire. Every mountain has many stories (no pun intended) and at least one storyteller to keep the legends alive. A few people still remember Roy Dudley, the first ranger at Katahdin's Chimney Pond, who introduced a generation of children and adults to Pamola in the 1930s. Roy often camped near the pond, twenty years before anyone thought seriously of making the area a public park. Without knowing it, Dudley was a pioneer of modern outdoor recreation. He built his

home under what he called "the sheltering rock," a flat slab of granite shaped naturally like a lean-to. Sure enough, the spirit of Pamola
swooped down to chase him away, but Roy refused to budge.

One day Roy walked to the pond to fetch some water for his
morning tea. Just as he was scooping up a bucketful of cold, clear
pond water, there came a great splash, as if a big fish had jumped
clear out of the pond, soaking Roy to the bone. Now he knew for a
fact there were no fish in Chimney Pond, so he looked up, and there
was Pamola, ugly as sin, standing on the Knife Edge with a five-foot
boulder in each hand. "You!" shouted Pamola. "Get off my mountain!
This is my mountain!" Pamola's voice was like the breath of winter.
In a moment the temperature dropped to near freezing, and the tall
pines trembled in the wind all across the basin. Down splashed the
first boulder, and half the water in Chimney Pond leapt up so high
that it came down as rain. Then Pamola hurled the second boulder,
and this one emptied the pond. By now, Pamola's breath had made
the air so cold that it started to snow. And it kept on snowing till it
refilled Chimney Pond. The ice didn't melt for three more days. Roy
gave up on tea and made some hot chocolate instead.

Jane Thomas was one of the children who listened to Roy
around those long-ago campfires. Now white-haired and in her
sixties, she's a member of the Baxter State Park Authority's advi-
sory committee. She is the storyteller now. A tan-colored ranger's
shirt is draped loosely over her shoulders like a coat. She sits in
a cabin at Daicey Pond with an audience of children spellbound
around her on the floor. Their parents, in chairs, are equally fascinated as Thomas tells them the stories of how Pamola slashed open
the great gash in Pamola Peak, how every month he crept out of
his cave and helped roll the full moon across the crags of the Knife
Edge to South Peak so it wouldn't get stuck.

"When the legislature established a game preserve here in 1917,
Roy Dudley was hired as a game warden," she says. "I guess they
thought it takes one to catch one. Roy was a pretty good poacher
himself." Roy was also legendary for his tea. "That tea would take
the bottom right out of an aluminum cup," laughs Thomas.

She talks about the grudging respect that grew between Pamola and Dudley. Over the years they became friends, and Roy taught Pamola to smoke a pipe. One night Pamola neglected his duty and left the moon to stumble across the rocks on its own. "It did pretty well for a while, bouncing along over the boulders—I've seen it do this myself." She's about to tell how the moon slipped and got stuck, and how Roy had to climb up to Pamola Peak and talk his friend out of his cave, when one of the children leaps up and points to the window.

A murmur rushes through the cabin. Outside, a rainbow rises out of the forest—a band of color shooting straight up through Katahdin, dividing the mountain in half. Miles high, the rainbow veers off to the right in a slow curve and blends with the mist. It glows a wide bright yellow, thinly lined with the rest of the colors of the spectrum. Everyone rushes outside, gazing at the mountain and the rainbow. The storyteller follows, her hands tucked in her pockets, and the moon is left stuck in the rocks. "I think Pamola likes it when I tell stories about him," she whispers to a parent, "'cause I've had the best luck with weather."

No one has seen Pamola since 1942, when Roy Dudley tried to hitch a ride from his off-season home in nearby Stacyville and was killed under the wheels of a logging truck.

People expect different things from the wilderness. Some seek recreation or inspiration. Some hunt for food or fun; others cut logs for profit. Some, like Pamola, just want to be left alone.

In 1976, forty-six Penobscot, Passamaquoddy, Micmac, and Maliseet Indians illegally invaded Baxter State Park and occupied Abol Campground at the foot of the "Greatest Mountain," Katahdin. Early one morning, they gunned a van full of Indian warriors through the gate when no one was looking. The invaders wanted the mountain and the lands in its shadow free of whites, to live in, to farm.

"The Indians intend to cut down trees and clear an area for settlement, then live there permanently, away from white society," announced their lawyer, Thomas Tureen. They cared not one whit about the law's ban on hunting or on permanent human settlement. Instead, they trusted themselves to kill what they needed, not to hunt a species to extinction.

In nearby towns, meanwhile, the reaction was relatively unperturbed. "If people from away are permitted to use the park, there's nothing wrong with Indians staying there," mumbled one man in Millinocket.

Governor Percival Baxter once said, "I want this mountain and this land left unimproved by man, as it was in the days when Indians lived in the woods"—but the Indians never did live there, not really. They lived to the south and roamed north only to hunt moose. Nor would Baxter have approved of their plan to use his park in 1976. They imported cars, beer and cigarettes, guns and knives. That was not the wilderness Baxter had in mind.

The beer-guzzling, smoking, car-driving Abenakis of 1976 simply did not behave like the quaint American Indians of legend. They didn't waltz naked through the woods or "go native." In many ways they resembled the "degraded savage" for whom Thoreau spared some poisonous words on his trip back from Katahdin in 1846.

"There is," said the bean farmer from Concord, "a remarkable and unexpected resemblance between the degraded savage and the lowest classes in a great city. The one is no more a child of nature than the other."

Thoreau thus described Louis Neptune, the same Penobscot who had saved geologist Charles Jackson's expedition in 1837, but who snubbed Thoreau and refused to guide him. Meeting Neptune on the river after his trip had ended, Thoreau struck out with angry words: "We thought Indians had some honor before. . . . Met face to face, these Indians in their native woods looked like the sinister and slouching fellows whom you meet picking up strings and paper in the streets of a city."

How odd it is to hear a white man call a Native American "degraded" when the Native American has simply adopted the white man's lifestyle. At first, Thoreau failed to recognize Neptune because the Indian was wearing a broad-brimmed hat, overcoat, and cape, "the spoils of Bangor." True Indians, apparently, were expected to endure the sun in their eyes, or stick feathers in their hair, or else never emerge from the shady trees.

While it may not be fair to Thoreau to focus on a single passage, especially not this tirade against an employee who failed to show up for work, the Sage of Concord does merit a posthumous slap on the wrist. Louis Neptune was clearly an able woodsman—hat or no hat.

What Thoreau has done in this passage is to define nature as the antithesis of civilization, as if you cannot have one without completely shedding the other—an argument he later disavowed in *Walden* and other writings. His words to the Indian were a slip, a mistake, a brief return to the guilt—shared by many—that makes us exclude ourselves from the natural world.

I believe wilderness is a presence of a wide variety of life, with all of these separate forms of life bound together in a loose knot; no one form dominates the others. The reason New York's Central Park is not a wilderness is that its trees and shrubs and squirrels and birds have been shaped and pruned by the city that surrounds them. Humans no longer simply interact; they determine. For the same reason, an ant colony, in and of itself, is not a wilderness. It is a city of ants, with every tunnel, every dirt-walled chamber built by and for a single species. A ladybug loose in the tunnels of an anthill is as lost and as short-lived as a moose in Manhattan. But an anthill in the lowlands of Baxter State Park is not an entity in itself. It is still a small, vital portion of the surrounding landscape. The ants must leave their home to forage in the world outside. So must we.

Today I seek the wilderness, but I bring the tools of civilization with me. An aluminum cup strapped to my pack rattles against the metal canteen inside. Each step I take, hopping boulder to boulder down the trail, produces a percussive slap; cup smacks canteen. I pause, stuffing the cup into an open pocket. As if to fill the sudden silence, my stomach grumbles. I reach for a granola bar. Overhead in a spruce tree, a chickadee whistles three crisp notes.

I am walking back from Chimney Pond on a chilly July afternoon; my knees ache. Up ahead, two hikers stop to watch a moose somewhere deep in the trees. They point, and I look, but the forest grows too thick. I see shades of green, dark ferns and light ferns, patches of blueberries and raspberries, the trunks of trees, and flashes of white birch bark that spice the dark growth. But no moose. The two insist on pointing. They need, it seems, to show me a moose; it is rude even to think of leaving. Who, after all, ignores moose? It is to see these giant, awkward creatures that tourists come to Maine.

More hikers catch up with us and they, too, stand in the growing audience, watching two strangers point at the invisible moose. Finally, disturbed by the crowd watching its nap, the animal stands up and walks away. Or that's what they tell me. I see only a glimpse of dark hide, a shadow moving amid other shadows, a fleeting presence.

A boy about ten years old stands aside from the crowd of sightseers. He is chubby and wears glasses, squinting down at the rocks so as not to stumble. While the adults search for invisible moose, he gathers a wreath of ferns. Now, one by one, he drops them in the inch-deep waters of a stream.

A bit of the ancient past lingers in ferns, as if memories from the dead age of dinosaurs sit forgotten in a small frond at the base of a modern-day oak tree. In ferns resides the quiet simplicity of earlier times when all the world was dark green. Sixty-five million years have passed since the last great reptile stood on the earth. Since then the continents have slid farther apart, the once-open plains have filled with trees, and the evolution of flowering plants has brought color to the land. Spore-bearing ferns have become an anachronism on a planet of fruit trees, a relic in an age of apples and berries.

Ancient as they are, our modern-day ferns have existed for just a flicker of time compared to the granite bones of the Appalachian Range. Rap a knuckle on a boulder and listen. Since that rock formed, generations of trees have lived, died, and turned to soil, birthing the young forests of today. Perhaps we come to mountains to feel young, to know that we will always be young in places such as these.

In the northern lowlands sits a bedrock of shale laid down as sedimentary rock by a forgotten ocean more than five hundred million years ago. Trapped inside the shale are tiny cavities shaped like life. Long ago, small beings swam in the ancient sea, deprived of minds and often of eyes. If they saw at all, it was a blurry world of shades of light and dark. Now all that is left of these beings are ghostly impressions in the rocks. The hikers and tourists who go there daily fix their eyes on distant hills; they step blindly on the ancient records of life embedded in the stones at their feet.

For all its grandeur, Katahdin is old and small. The serrated Knife Edge and the steep bowl of the Great Basin are new features carved out by the last of the glaciers, a mere ten to twelve thousand years ago. Sometimes, if you squint, these sharp and jagged features look like the high peaks of the Rockies—but it's all illusion. The true birth of these rocks and the entire Appalachian Range stretches back beyond the birth of the ferns, back to a time when the boulders that now lie crumbled and broken on the tablelands, four thousand feet above the sea, were a ball of molten magma boiling nine miles underground.

The birth of the Appalachian Mountains took place in a world with few colors; green and brown, gray rocks tinged red with rust. It was a world of giant continents pressing together and one giant ocean. A massive slab of granite that would become North America rubbed against the coastlines of what would one day be Europe and

Africa, and a mountain range was born. A chunk of Scotland fastened onto the New World while the rest of Europe slid away.

It happened more than three hundred million years ago, before the age of dinosaurs, not long after the first amphibious creature set foot on land and decided to stay.

Such a number—three hundred million years—is meaningless to a human mind. It's older, far older, than the earth's highest peaks. The Rockies are only sixty million years old, the Himalayas less than forty million. The last of the dinosaurs never lived to see the West Coast drift alongside the mainland, pushing up the Sierra Nevada, and the world had filled with mammals by the time the Indian subcontinent smashed into Asia. All these mountains are young, their highest peaks sharp and steep. They have a history of upheaval, of rolling glaciers, of colliding continents. This history is written in rocks, in ice that never melts, in crags thrust three miles high.

The mountains of New England hold in their past a history of decay, buried under soil and leaves, under cow pastures and cornfields. The scars left by the last glaciers have been obscured by ten thousand years of wind and rain. Entire mountains have been erased. All that remains is a range of low hills.

Human beings have started to make a mark on these ancient hills. On Doubletop, a steep peak just west of Katahdin, rests a relic of a man's life. A metal plate sits where it shouldn't be, fixed to the rocks like one of Floyd Neary's benchmarks. The plaque reads:

Keppele Hall June 10, 1872–April 25, 1926

My first encounter with Mr. Keppele Hall took place on a summer day when chill winds whistled through the trees. A rain cloud lunged at the mountain, impaling itself on the peak. Alone,

I had just pulled myself onto the summit, gripping the trunk of a stunted spruce tree. Flakes of moist bark crumbled in my hands. Roots like gnarled fingers dug into the soil. Finally, I stood and gazed into the inner belly of a cloud.

There was no view; the distant lakes and hills were gone, erased by the fog. But curiously, a breeze had brushed clear a yard or so of clear air, and in that open space I saw Keppele Hall. Or, rather, I saw his grave.

His name was inscribed there, stuck vertically to a boulder on the peak. I stepped closer, rubbing my fingertips against the grayish green surface. The plaque was rectangular, with a domed top. A six-pointed star glittered above his name, while the sketchy outline of a genie's lamp lay across the bottom. What, I wondered, was a grave doing on a mountaintop?

The plaque faces south, staring down at the Penobscot River and the distant logging town of Millinocket. To the east, mile-high Mount Katahdin hoists up the skyline. Waves of green hills ripple in its shadow. West of here, the reflective blue lakes of the Allagash sparkle and gleam.

Below Mr. Hall's name, the plaque offers a lament:

His ashes were given to the winds
at this place August 20, 1926,
at sunset, by his wife.
Love only is eternal.

Who was Keppele Hall, and what tragedy links him to this land forever? What is he doing here now, eighty years after his death, with a full view of Katahdin rising in the east like the sun?

Who was his wife, that remarkable, nameless woman who must have clawed her way up the slopes, carrying in her arms an urn, so that her husband's ashes could be scattered to the winds? Did she stay while the last glint of daylight sank behind the Allagash?

No one knows. The mountain stands where it has always stood, but it is unaware of Keppele Hall. Perhaps our human lifetimes are too brief, our visits too rare, and the aging hills do not register our presence at all.

Building a Mountain,
Taking It Down

angers at Baxter State Park still speak of Helen Ciaravino, the spry, gray-haired woman who once tested the strength of her seven decades against the unyielding granite of the tallest peak in Maine.

She was, she said, "no greenhorn." She already had section-hiked all but "a very few spots" along the Appalachian Trail, plus countless other peaks in her native state of Maine. To celebrate her seventy-fifth birthday she intended to climb the last stretch of the Appalachian Trail up Mount Katahdin, cross the perilous Knife Edge, and meet her husband, Casper, on the other side.

It was September then, when the autumn winds first brush the peaks. At a campground called Roaring Brook, Casper waited with their car, a sky blue Buick. She wanted no company for this trip. She brought nothing but a canteen, an extra sweater, and faded memories of the mountain, which she had climbed in her youth.

Helen slumped, scrambled, and rolled up the trail. On the highest pinnacle, she started to think about her age, about the hours of hard climbing and the four miles of steep, loose ground still to go. The clouds lowered. Fog wrapped around her, rain fell, and soon she was slipping on the wet rocks. At the start of an Ice Age arête called the Knife Edge, she faltered. Passersby asked if she needed help, if she was hurt. She announced that she could not possibly take another step today. Would someone please tell her husband?

A rescue team found her at nightfall, too late to climb back down. A temporary winter set in along with darkness. Pellets of sleet now bounced off the rocks. Black clouds crossed the sky. The temperature fell to thirty-eight degrees. Helen was dressed for summer, for daylight, and had to borrow a sleeping bag and plastic sheets from the rangers to prevent hypothermia. She endured an unpleasant night shivering in a makeshift shelter of rocks, while around her the wind roared like white water. In the morning, aided by rangers, she descended the mountain and turned seventy-five years old again.

Hearing Helen Ciaravino's story for the first time, I immediately imagined the experiences of my own sprightly ninety-year-old grandmother, who once broke her hip while scrambling over a fence at the base of Mount Katahdin. She, too, suddenly remembered her age. She came home to a tiny village in the woods, staying in a house with a view of the mountain to the north. The resolve that had powered her across the rocks now ebbed from her body. She leaned on a cane and was driven around town by a grandson to places where she used to walk. Lines and cracks multiplied on her face. On the distant horizon, the granite slopes still wait for her return, but never again will she climb Katahdin, or any mountain.

People are mortal, and it is the brevity of our stay on earth that makes mountains seem old. Stony and aloof, mountains endure while human generations rise and pass away in endless repetition.

Mount Katahdin's crags, eroded by rain and wind, jut sharply above a flat alpine meadow strewn with rocks and gnarled shrubs. These "tablelands," in turn, slope down to the north toward a shady, wooded land inhabited by moose and deer, fox and bear. By October, the ground in the lowlands is padded with brown leaves. But a mile higher the first frost of winter digs into cracks in the boulders, scratching out the erosive scars of yet another year.

Some hills, like Katahdin, are truly ancient. But many ranges are young, unfinished, a protrusion of rocky buds on the planet's surface. In the Sierras of California that environmentalist John Muir knew so well, steep peaks continue to rise, thrust to ever greater heights by the internal mechanisms of the Earth, too fast for erosion to wear them down.

Mountains, like people, are born and grow old, but they do so outside of our limited understanding of time. No human being has the ability to witness a mountain raised high, then leveled to a forested plain—no more than a bumblebee stranded on the high ridges can survive for a human lifetime. That bee, hiding in a niche from the cold winds of July, lacks the intelligence to measure time or notice its passing. It cannot predict that one day I will cease to exist. To an insect, doomed to die in a matter of days, I am as permanent as the mountain is to me.

"Two hundred years ago is about as great an antiquity as we can comprehend or often have to deal with," writes Henry David Thoreau. "It is nearly as good as two thousand to our imaginations. It carries us back to the days of aborigines and the Pilgrims; beyond the limits of oral testimony, to history which begins already to be enamelled with a gloss of fable."

If we can scarcely imagine two hundred years, how can we hope to comprehend two million? Two billion? Yet we must try, if we are to understand the formation of Katahdin.

No one lives to see a mountain go up, or come down. For time's greatest works we must rely on science and the evidence in the stones. Time molds stars and planets out of the dust of space, shapes rock into mountains in tens of millions of years. Insects, like the bee, it kills off in days or weeks. Woods replace a meadow in sixty years, while the dancing atoms trade electrons by the picosecond.

Our knowledge of time and its grip on the world has changed quickly and profoundly in recent years, as science has changed. No one thought to split a second into smaller units until we noticed the speed of the microscopic, subatomic world. There was no need to preface years with terms of millions or billions until geology knocked down the back door of our preconceptions, exposing a universe far older than anyone had ever dared to imagine. The modern theory of plate tectonics swallows time in great gulps; it sets islands adrift on the seas while sundered continents slowly press together, squeezing out the oceans in between. What was accepted in the nineteenth century—the old idea that hills wrinkle as the earth's skin cools and withdraws, like the peel of a shrunken fruit—is now known to be completely wrong. That theory has gone the way of atmospheric comets and spontaneous generation—maggots out of cheese and mice from old rags—ideas that avoid a need for the depths of time.

Books of science get shelved in dark, dusty corners sooner than other, more durable literary forms. Science is always changing, improving. No one wants a ten-year-old geology textbook, much less a dusty catalog of errors from the nineteenth century. Stores discard such books in bargain bins in the hope that catchy titles and a price tag of a dollar will get rid of them. Years later, the same texts reappear at lawn sales, stuffed into crates alongside yellow-paged novels from the 1930s, priced at fifty cents apiece.

Packed into a cardboard box in the attic of my grandmother's house is a book of astronomy, printed in the year I was born. The book counts ten moons in orbit around Saturn, ranks Pluto as twice the size of Mercury, and confidently proclaims the probable existence of life on Mars. Like most textbooks it's patronizing, simplified, and difficult to read, deserving of its exile in the attic; but for a few years the errors it listed as facts could not be proven wrong. Next to it, a book on paleontology, cast away by a friend who had lost all interest in fossils, puts the creation of life just below the Cambrian-Precambrian boundary, 570 million years ago—a guess that misses the mark by several billion years.

Suppose a publisher, eager to market a scientific history of the earth, came up with a new ploy: a reference book that covers in a single volume the entire history of the earth, from the ignition of the sun to the waning years of the twentieth century and beyond. Imagine that this book divides the earth's history into segments of one million years, one segment per page. The book would run to nearly five thousand pages, a hefty tome. By necessity, recent events like the European Renaissance or political revolutions in the United States and France are largely ignored. The "Age of Mammals," however, occupies a sizable chapter. Even the story of *Homo sapiens* and their forebears, needing millions of years to lift their front paws off the ground and stand erect, takes a page or two to tell. Billions of years of evolution—of mountain ranges, continents, and the sudden explosion of complex life—are condensed into a story that can be held (with some difficulty) in one's own hands.

No such book exists, of course. If it did, the last page would overflow with details in microscopic print, and even those chapters stretching back hundreds of millions of years would need to be summaries in order to be legible. Even with the current gaps in our knowledge, there is simply too much data to fit in a book of everything. Imagine trying to read the entire contents of the Library of Congress, or the genetic code on a million double helixes of DNA. Neither task is easy, or likely. But the idea of such a book—to condense the story of the world to a single text—serves a point. To get a grip on deep time, to sense and understand epochs of millions of years that the dials of our clocks cannot possibly measure, it's easiest to think of time as a metaphor.

A majority of our book's pages are blank, or nearly so; we have not yet uncovered enough evidence to fill them all. The pages stare back at us, white and empty, a mockery of human ignorance. There exist too many millions of years about which we know little or nothing. Browse casually; glance at page after page of blank sheets, occasionally interrupted by stabs of facts in black ink—it's a humbling experience. To get a feel for the enormity of time, a reader should turn the pages one by one and spend a full minute on each, even the empty ones.

Fifteen hours crawl by before the first mention of life; less than four days later the entire story is over. If a reader pauses to eat or sleep or go to work in the morning, the experience can stretch into a week, a month, or longer—an eon, an eternity. Who, given freedom of choice, could stare at white paper continuously for a week? Who could concentrate for so long?

Albert Einstein—a relatively good scientist—tells us that time is just one more dimension, like up or down or sideways. Time is relative. "How long is a long time?" I wonder. The answer: "It depends."

If a white pine tree, spared by fire and disease, also escapes a death by chainsaw, it may live over three hundred years. Today's saplings will live to witness the quintcentennial of the United States. Hemlocks live even longer, five to six hundred years; other species of spruce and pine, two hundred fifty years at best. Hardwoods die sooner, and the thick golden birches prominent throughout the woods of Maine grow old by their two-hundredth year. The common paper birch seldom survives as long as a century.

Ancient hemlocks cluster in isolated groves around Mount Katahdin, in places too steep or remote for the timber corporations to haul their equipment. They were alive when French trappers canoed down the Allagash and Saint John rivers to trap furs. In 1837 these very trees stood tall—mature—while the surveyor Charles Jackson climbed atop the highest peak in Maine and waved his barometer in defiance of Pamola.

Trees live to ancient years on the human scale, but it is still a span of time within our grasp. An old grandfather is a fraction of the age of an old tree, but a reasonable fraction: a quarter, a half. The most ancient living being on earth is a tree that sprouted many millennia before the primitive tribes on the Italian Peninsula organized themselves into the Roman Empire and conquered all of Europe. The estimated age limit of macrozamia trees in Australia is twelve thousand years, but they are a cycad species that does not grow rings, so the dating is imprecise. The oldest authenticated giant redwood in California has 3,200 rings, but there is a bristlecone pine in California's White Mountains that tops even that number; it is 4,600 years old. African baobabs and Indian banyan trees are known to possess a similar longevity.

The oldest human on record lived to a mere 122 years. Across the globe, typical lifespans range from four decades in poverty-stricken Chad to over eighty years in Japan.

Henry David Thoreau died of tuberculosis at age forty-four. Coughing on his deathbed, the last words he mumbled to his sister were "moose, Indians," recalling fond memories of his trips to Maine.

The mountains of Maine are part of the Appalachian Range, a two-thousand-mile ridge of mostly Paleozoic rock, born in a period of tectonic activity lasting a hundred million years, continuing as the first forms of complex life on earth were born in the ocean and in time began to creep, crawl, or waft onto shore with the winds.

In 1846, while Henry David Thoreau was fretting about ghosts and fog on Mount Katahdin, paleontologists on both sides of the Atlantic were busily unearthing trilobite fossils from limestone and shale. Today, even people who cannot define the word paleontology or are unused to thinking about deep time can often point to and name the figures of trilobites. These thumb- or hand-sized shelled animals that once scurried in primordial waters are now fossilized collector's items; replicas serve as paperweights and museum gift shop keepsakes.

Trilobites are ancient, alien, yet somehow they look familiar to us. They have eyes—fossils that stare back at us, peering out of the Cambrian era. Those eyes were made of calcite and did not see the world as we see it, but they were suggestive of more evolution to come. Long after the time trilobites flourished, five hundred million years ago, other simple marine animals—brachiopods, mollusks, nautiloids—were dying on the sediment-covered floors of ancient seas that would one day turn to stone. Their shapes were forever embedded in sandstone and mud.

In western Maine a buildup of soil, sand, and stone has eroded from the underlying bedrock near the hamlet of Eustis. Exposed to wind and rain after an eon underground, here lie the oldest rocks known to exist in this corner of the world. They are aged a modest 1.6 billion years, about a third as old as the earth itself. The rock is coarse-grained gneiss, born in an era when the land was lifeless, when simple blue-green algae and microscopic organisms in the waters pumped a trickle of oxygen into the air. Canadian outcrops near Hudson Bay and in central Canada expose a bedrock that reaches even farther back in time. The oldest, rarest rocks found on earth formed nearly four billion years ago—roughly the same age as stone taken off the tectonically dead surface of the moon by Apollo astronauts.

Four billion years. The span of time between then and now deserves more than the scant praise of an "eon," or "a long time," but our language lacks a word for it. Humans, as a species, have not thought on such a scale until now.

Do we really feel the difference between a million and a billion? Does one billion six hundred million years mean anything real to us? What about three hundred sixty million years, the age of Katahdin's granite? Or forty million, the age of the Himalayas? Try to imagine just six million years, the span of time during which the Colorado River has busily carved out the Grand Canyon.

Even a million years is an eternity—time enough for humanity to make tools and discover fire, for civilizations to rise in seemingly endless repetition, for our present technology to hurl a spacecraft to a nearby solar system—but far too brief a time to build a mountain or take it down.

One billion years is long enough to construct a dozen mountain ranges and destroy them all, or to exhaust the thermonuclear engines of a star. A million, a billion—they both qualify as a long time, but on different scales, just as to us ninety-three years is lengthy on the more familiar human scale.

Years obviously fail as a unit of measure when talking about geology or astronomy. There's nothing to grip; the years pour through our fingers. Listing the earth's age in years is as unreasonable as counting the time till Christmas in seconds rather than days. Can we sense a difference between 31 million seconds and 3.1 million? Is it a matter of minutes, hours, days, or years?

Calculating the answer is a simple task, but few feel it instinctively. Thirty-one million seconds puts Christmas a full year away. When there are 3.1 million seconds to go, it is already late November. Signs begin to appear in toy-store windows by mid-December: "Hurry! Only one million shopping seconds left!"

Turning the pages of an imaginary book to represent epochs in earth's history, as I did earlier, is an imperfect metaphor. Our brains still reject the enormity of deep time. A more familiar and perhaps more understandable analogy requires us to turn instead the pages of a calendar.

The idea that all of time should be shoved, squeezed, and reduced to a metaphorical year is not a new one. The late astronomer Carl Sagan displayed an affection for eternity; he used the analogy in his treatise on the evolution of intelligence, *The Dragons of Eden*. On his scale, the earth forms in mid-September, primitive life in October, and mammals only in the last few days of the year.

A year is a frame of reference we can understand. But it is too short as a model. Perhaps a century would serve us better. That would put a few minutes between such important events as the fall of Rome and the fall of the Berlin Wall. The only problem is that a metaphorical century is too large; it is a scale bigger than ourselves. A year will have to do.

Carl Sagan's year starts at the very beginning of time, the Big Bang. But I am not so ambitious. To make the metaphor practical, it's necessary to truncate time. Remove the "silent" ten or so billion years prior to the creation of earth. Start the year with the origin of the earth, at a time when the universe itself was already unfathomably old. On such a scale, a single day encompasses more than 12.5 million years. Every minute of that day equals slightly more than 8,700 years. A second is nearly a century and a half.

If we place the formation of the earth on January first, the Big Bang is already several years old. Life—small single-celled organisms, our ancestors—appears in the muck of late February and early March. No one knows for certain when the spark of life first flashes in Darwin's "warm little pond." But one thing we do know*: It stays simple for billions of years. Not until mid-November do the trilobites emerge. With the Cambrian explosion, we see a profusion of creatures with shells—brachiopods, echinoderms, and nautiloids. Some have eyes to look out at the world. Plants start to take root on shore, but no animals yet emerge from out of the sea. The atmosphere by this point is growing rich in oxygen.

By Thanksgiving and for about a week thereafter, while Iapetus—the precursor of the Atlantic Ocean—is closing, islands smash against the North American coast. Plants colonize the land; fossils continue to be laid down in sedimentary rocks at the bottom

---

* Or do we? Perhaps in another twenty years the reference books of today will seem just as quaint and incomplete as the obsolete astronomy book I mentioned earlier. Our knowledge is always evolving as we observe and learn more about the universe. The ability to correct errors and to constantly reevaluate, improve, and expand on our ideas in the light of new evidence is science's great strength—and the reason old science books sell so cheaply.

of ancient seas. The bulbs of rhyolite that now form Traveler Mountain spill onto the surface on November 26, 440 million years ago. A few days later, Katahdin granite intrudes deep underground. The sea washes away; continents merge, then pull apart. Finally, the Atlantic Ocean is born near the start of the Mesozoic Era, 245 million years ago; it is now the second week of December. At various points during the next two weeks we see evidence of tropical rain forests in Connecticut. The footprints of dinosaurs lope across southern New England. Out in the west, the oldest of the rocks that someday will make up the Grand Canyon are already locked in place, though of course the Colorado River does not yet exist. Nor do the Rocky Mountains.

Old mountains erode and new ones rise to take their places as the metaphorical calendar flips from week to week, day to day. The spread of flowering plants occurs on or about December 21 — the winter solstice, by remarkable coincidence. The beginning of the Cenozoic Era, the age of mammals, falls on the day after Christmas, shortly after the catastrophe that extinguished the dinosaurs. Mammals crawl out of the shadows into daylight unchallenged. Glaciers etch the last fine sculpture work on the mountains of New England two minutes before the end of the year; Troy falls at 11:59:39 PM. Henry David Thoreau wraps himself in clouds on Katahdin a second before the clock ticks over into a new year.

I glance at my wristwatch and see that time is moving at the familiar human pace. I am halfway up Katahdin, but the sky has closed in and I can proceed no farther. Piece by piece the fog is taking the mountain away. Occasionally the fog around me thins to a wispy white film, letting in sunlight, and I am able to walk quickly to the next visible cairn. Other times the fog is a dark gray soup, impassible. I cannot see the trail and must wait.

A sudden cracking, crashing sound echoes just ahead. It sounds like boulders set rolling, as if some giant creature has stumbled. Immediately I think of moose—but no, surely I am up too high. There is little for moose to eat up here. Whatever made the noise was not a hiker, for I hear no talking, no self-deprecatory curses or cries for help. But someone—or something—is out there.

When the clouds slide off again, I see nothing but barren land. The granite looks the same as ever. There is no moose, no bear, no party of hikers climbing over the mountain. But something must have caused that noise—unless it was Pamola himself stepping down out of a patch of cloud and dying like an old myth in the sunlight.

I think I know the answer. The mountain shifted. For a thousand years, a loose rock poised on a ledge while wind and ice and the feet of moose, deer, caribou, and fox shook it off its base. That rock may have been waiting to fall for a hundred millennia. At last, a final nudge of wind dropped it down on a rock just below—a crack, the sound of a mountain coming down, inch by inch by inch. That rock will wait for millennia before it moves again.

The land looks no different than a minute ago, but I have heard it crumbling, ever so gradually. A slab of rock slides a single inch closer to the sea. Across the tablelands, across the eons, the process repeats. Too slowly to notice, a river of rocks is flowing down these slopes into the flat forest below. That is the speed of a mountain coming down. It is ancient yet mortal.

Rural Places

A small, lean man sits in the bow of his canoe, swaying to and fro as waves lap at the birch bark. His face is calm, thoughtful. His name is Henry Thoreau. Behind him his guide, a Penobscot Indian called Joe Aitteon, slaps a paddle on the water, propelling their boat away from shore.

Nearby, a trout leaps and splashes its tail on the water; Thoreau blinks in surprise. Two loons greet the dawn with a cry, a shiver of sound. Pieces of the sun sparkle and glitter, scattered across the lake like a fire's embers.

The lake is Moosehead Lake, Maine. The year is 1853. Far to the north, Mount Katahdin stands on the horizon. Thoreau glances at it, his first glimpse of the mountain since his ordeal in the clouds seven years earlier. He turns away quickly, looking back toward shore. Something is lying there—a pair of moose antlers on the beach. "I asked Joe if a moose had shed them," he writes, "but he said there was a head attached to them, and I knew that they did not shed their heads more than once in their lives."

A witty fellow, Mr. Thoreau. He was always happiest on rivers or lakes, or deep in the forest, rather than standing atop one of the hills of New England, which some people call mountains. In his journal, he calls the North Woods "that stuff we hear of in Massachusetts"—rolling, treeish, unfettered, and free.

We hear of "that stuff" back in New York State, too. We even see it, though farther south our forest is creased with highways. Perhaps the intrusion of strips of blacktop makes the Adirondacks or Catskills a lesser wilderness, but if so, we see more of that lesser wilderness than most natives of Maine—or Alaska or Montana or any timber country—see of their vast pure one. We cannot help but see it; we drive through it every day. In summer there are leafy trees, in spring a thaw, an odor of farms, of cut alfalfa and bits of hay chaff floating in the breeze. Autumn leaves rain down on cars. In winter, boughs of evergreens sag into the roads, shutting them in, turning wide thoroughfares small and countrylike, walled in by snow.

In the dairy lands of upstate New York, where I was born, cornfields nestle in the pockets of the hills. The logging counties of central Maine lack them. On the outskirts of a timber town in the land Thoreau once visited, I see only pillars of trees—familiar firs and spruces. A narrow strip of forest stands alongside every road, left uncut by law. The state legislature has declared such a buffer zone necessary for scenic purposes—a logical decision in a state financed by tourism. An ugly field of stumps might exist just beyond the buffer, but from the road it's impossible to tell. Maine's crop is spruce and pine, its products paper and lumber. New York State's farm country produces milk and cheese. Both states are rural. They are practically neighbors, tucked in a crowded corner of the map with tiny rectangular states on their borders. Twenty thousand years ago, while the Adirondack Mountains sagged beneath millions of tons of ice, valley glaciers were busy carving out basins on Mount Katahdin. Ten thousand years later, the ice sheets melted in both regions.

Today, rural Maine and rural New York lack the pollution of city lights, enjoying natural darkness in which the stars are sharp and clear as diamonds. Both states invite populations of "summer people," owners of fine houses who visit in July and August, but leave their mansions empty when the air turns cold or business calls them away. Rundown motels with peeling paint offer housing for less affluent tourists.

In early October, in the land where I was born, wind combs through the stubble of alfalfa on the fields. Fog broods in valleys and meadows, while morning dew clings to cornstalks. I feel the bite of wind on my skin, see a threat of snow in low, gray clouds. A crescent moon drags through the trees; its light slices through the branches of maples and pines. The maple leaves are red, orange, and gold. But already the upper branches are bare; halos of fallen leaves circle the tree trunks. Oaks are the most possessive trees, holding onto their leaves the longest as they turn a dull red brown. By mid-October the naked birches have shed their leaves and must poke and prod the sky like spears.

In farm country, autumn is a season for slowing down. The last hay gets stacked in barns. The first snow squalls whiten the ground. Melodies of birds in the trees fade, note by note, as the musicians fly away. By November the hills, valleys, and streams seem to slip into a sleep that will last until spring.

In any season, New York State is a land of winding roads, farms, and small towns. Tractor tires cut ribbons in the black dirt of the fields, and grazing cows lift their heads to stare dully at an occasional passing car. Timber country has no grazing cows. A great forest borders the northern villages. It's possible (or so it seems) to slip under the canopy and never again feel the sun, not even if you walk a hundred miles north to Canada. Bear and moose lurk in the shadows nearby, unseen, curiously eyeing the brightly painted houses, listening to the diesel growl of trucks' engines and the shouts of children. Boughs of conifers and hardwoods stretch over the roads, dropping seeds and cones onto rooftops.

A land accessible from a parking lot quickly tramples its wild nature under the treads of hiking boots and rubber tires. Car doors slam shut, keys turn in the locks. Children frolic around the campground, playing hide and seek in a field of boulders, too impatient to wait for Mom and Dad to pitch the tent. Yet beneath the noise you still can hear the trills of sparrows and the mad cackle of loons.

Wilderness is too often defined as an absence of humanity. A farm is not wilderness because its land is tamed by the farmer. Plants grow in straight rows, no longer wild. Animals are fenced in, or caged, dependent on people for their food and water. Even a distant, unused clearing, far back in the hills, fails as wilderness; its weeds and grasses are cordoned off by an unnatural rectangle of trees. Seldom-used dirt roads that vanish under sprouting grass in the fall are turned back to road by tractor tires in the spring.

Wilderness has become a fetish for people dissatisfied with the smog of cities. It's supposed to be somehow purer than we citified, civilized humans are, eagerly sought by those in need of spiritual healing—though some would argue that humans, too, are a part of the natural world. We belong to the wilderness, they say, not the other way round.

An accurate definition of wilderness is hard to come by. Is it like Maine: An uninterrupted forest in which moose and bear roam freely until the paper company chooses to cut a swath through the trees, forcing them to move? Is it like rural New York: A land lined with small roads, dotted with tiny villages, where trees that are standing live for centuries but hang their boughs over roads, which purr with the engines of cars?

It's possible to drive for hours in the hills where I was born and never see another vehicle, unless one is at rest on the gravel-packed driveway of someone's home. One county route dwindles from a well-packed dirt road into two small gutters for the tires, with a strip of tall grass up the middle. Tree trunks form a wall on either side, so there is no room for two cars to pass. Overhead the branches criss-cross and make a wooden roof; the road becomes a tunnel with a circle of sky at the end but no light overhead. It's dim enough that I cannot see without headlights. This, at four in the afternoon.

Moments later the strip connects with a paved road. The canopy parts to reveal a bright blue sky. Both roads are empty.

Should I feel guilty for burning gas and spilling fumes out my car's exhaust pipe while I enjoy the wilderness? Maybe. Like the thousands of backpackers, sightseers, and hunters who throng in the woods in spring, summer, and autumn, I don't want people telling me I can't do it—and yet, if I were the only one doing it, the noise, the crowds, and the trampled trails wouldn't be a problem. But all of America likes to drive. If everyone chose a sunny afternoon to visit the mountains, such leisurely sightseeing drives would cease to be a pleasure.

It's hard to call the Adirondacks or New York's farm country artificial or human corrupted when the human presence is so weak. On this road, a human artifact, I have seen many thousands of trees, a hundred finches and jays, but only two people. From thirty yards off the road the people could not have been seen, and even the rattle of their cars might have been drowned by the gurgling of a stream.

Roads crisscross the woods, though they are small, seldom traveled. Trees stand closely packed on the edges. There are clearings sometimes, for towns or isolated farmhouses, but these are boxed in by the trees. If this is a wilderness, it's an accessible one; it includes people.

Our guilt in harming the environment makes us try to exclude ourselves from it. This is a mistake. If we define wilderness as the complete absence of people, then there is no wilderness left in the contiguous United States. There's nowhere to go, however remote, without finding some small trace of human existence. It might be a footpath through the woods, or the moldy skeleton of a two-hundred-year-old barn, or the flat stump of an old tree cut down by a chainsaw on state land. Even on the lonely summit of Katahdin, rising out of the greenness and the lakes that spread for hundreds of miles, a tiny puff of smoke wafting from the paper mill in the nearest human settlement is visible, twenty-five miles away.

A tourist from Rhode Island—a round-faced giant of a man, dressed in blue jeans that barely make it down to his feet—summed up Millinocket this way: "It's a small town, with all the disadvantages of a small town, and some of the disadvantages of a big one." He drags the last puff from his cigarette, drops the stump on the pavement of Penobscot Avenue, and squashes it with his foot.

Katahdin stands black and grim in the north, wrapped in clouds. He looks at it wistfully. It's a sunny day in Millinocket. "I mean, for city folk it's a normal small town. No movies, hardly any stores, no nightlife to speak of." He hardly needs to say it; he wants to climb the mountain. That's what brought him here in the first place. But the town itself is a disappointment. Penobscot Avenue, the business district, points nearly directly at Katahdin, but its aim is slightly off; it points too far north. From a distance and a height, a shoulder of Katahdin seems to rest on Newberry's Department Store, while the rest of the mountain embraces Epstein's Shoes.

The comment about "big towns" is left unexplained. I already know what he means. Alcoholism is a problem. "Millinocket has the number one use of alcohol of any city in the country," boasts a freckle-faced native, age thirteen. He scratches his curly haired head and smiles, oddly proud of the fact. Out by East Millinocket, a rundown bar alongside Route 11 offers up beer and a striptease on Saturday nights. "Girls! Girls! Girls!" a sign declares.

Older residents don't mention alcoholism or topless bars, except in off-color jokes. But they do complain about the noise and the clogged traffic, the inevitable result of having only one real road.

There's a shortcut, but only one. Everyone knows the shortcut; everyone uses it. At times, the main route becomes the shorter cut, the shortcut a traffic jam.

I feel alien in northern Maine. These roads are not my roads. A lumber truck roaring down Route 11 has a stacked, denuded forest trailing from its bed. More trucks follow. Pickup trucks packed with gun racks—empty for the summer—prowl everywhere: Route 11, I-95, the side streets. This breed of motorist is a familiar sight in the Adirondacks and dairy lands of New York and ought comfortably to remind me of home, but it doesn't. I don't belong to this clan, cannot belong, even though I come from an equally rural—perhaps more rural—region not far away. I could protest, shout, "Hey! I grew up in a small town, too. I know what it's like." But no one would listen. I am a "furriner" by birth—a New Yorker.

The people of Maine sport a clannish pride like nowhere else in the country—except, perhaps, Texas. "I've been in New York now thirty years and I still consider myself from Maine," says a native, my mother. It's tempting to call her a former native, but in Maine that attitude doesn't wash. Her pedigree is unassailable, like a tattoo that will never wash away; she is always welcome back.

"When new people move in, if they happen to do something a little different—well, it's because they're from away. It takes time to be accepted." By time, she means generations. Even the children of people from away—transplanted Down Easters—are still considered strangers, no matter if they were born in Maine and never once set foot outside. They bear the burden of their parents' blood.

Another native chimes in: "If a cat has kittens in an oven, do you call them biscuits?"

"Which way to Millinocket?"—"You can't get there from here," runs an old joke. Deep in these woods, no one is likely to ask me for directions to Lake Placid, New York, though I could tell them how to get there. If a tourist asked me which way to Mattawamkeag, I wouldn't know, except to point vaguely to the east.

Native human beings, like native deer or moose, are not hard to find in northern counties with aboriginal names: Penobscot, Aroostook, Piscataquis County. Just close your eyes and walk in a straight line, and you are likely to bump into one before long. But outsiders are missing, except in places where they are supposed to go: the parks, motels, and colleges. A quick examination of the parking lot at Roaring Brook Campground finds a cluster of out-of-state license plates that easily outnumbers the decorative lobster plates of Maine. But go just thirty miles southeast to Millinocket, to an acre of potholes, puddles, and mud in front of Ames department store and IGA groceries, and search for a sign of New Jersey, New York, or Connecticut. Where are all the tourists? Somehow they get to the park and trailheads by the hundreds. Do they pass magically through the air?

Drive with a stranger down an obscure rural street, or enter a small town far outside the usual tourist routes—you will feel watched. The roads lead nowhere; there is no good reason for a stranger to follow them. The people keep an eye on you, let you know you are out of place—until they discover which relative you belong to, and then the sheer numbers of their invitations and goodwill must politely be warded off.

Visitor is a just a kinder word for stranger, for foreigner, a ploy often used by natives in tourist-infested regions. Ordinarily, people are visitors while they pay and strangers once the door closes behind them. It's not that rural folk instantly dislike travelers. They just know that strangers will always stay strangers. It's necessary to keep aloof; there's no reason not to. That doesn't rule out friendliness toward people from away, but it's a surface friendliness, easily scratched.

The driver of an overcrowded station wagon who asks, "Which way to the beach?" of a fisherman in Bar Harbor, Maine, will never get to know that fisherman well, never reach the point where he may be confided in or trusted. Most likely, the tourist will say "Thank you" and never be seen again—and good riddance. Tourists emerge from the same mold; you have to look very closely to find a particular individual. And you have to care enough to look.

Tourists ask the same questions, want to see the same sights, and never stay in one place long enough to flesh out their characters or reveal personalities and interests that distinguish them from other transients. "I think they should blow up the Kittery Bridge," said one Mainer, when told of the state's plans to "encourage" natives to smile more at visitors. "Keep those people down in Boston where they belong." (I replied that blowing up the bridge was unlikely ever to happen. After all, no Maine is an island.)

No one likes a tourist. It's one of the pleasures of being rustic, to chew on a piece of straw and laugh at the odd ways of strangers, to give directions to the lost, to feel pity for pouting children strapped to the backseat of a car for what you know—but they don't—will be a long and bumpy ride. The bridge is under construction, and you tell them this and provide a complicated, alternate route that dodges through the cornfields and over the river. But they almost certainly will forget the route along the way—and may even have forgotten it in the telling.

That's all right—they can't get there from here, anyway.

Population growth and suburban sprawl have become front-burner issues in recent years. Visitors to Yellowstone, Yosemite, and other state and national parks are sometimes more likely to see traffic jams than wildlife, until they stray from the beaten path.

Far from designated wilderness areas, the traditional rivalry between urban and rural communities has been exacerbated as suburban sprawl changes both the landscape and the attitudes of the people who live there. "There's a lot of concern in Iowa and beyond that you have more and more people coming to rural America who think food comes from the supermarket, not the farm," reported USA Today in 1999. "If we really want to protect the right to farm, we have to make sure there's land to farm on."

Across the United States an increasing number of lawsuits and complaints are filed every year by one-time city dwellers who move to the country for the peace and quiet and the scenery, only to be dismayed by the odors and noises of neighboring farms. One farmer was successfully sued for "trespass" when smoke from his fields drifted across a new neighbor's property. ("There are certain operations that have to be done when they have to be done," explained another farmer. "You can't wait for a rainstorm to settle the dust.") In February 1999 the Supreme Court rejected an Iowa law protecting farmers from so-called nuisance lawsuits. Similar "right to farm" laws are now under review in all fifty states.

In turn, farmers and longtime rural residents resent the newcomers who try to change their traditional way of life, changing the way the landscape and its natural resources may be used in the process. "If you move out to the country, you need to accept that that's what you're doing," said Oregon farmer JoAnn Hathaway in 1998.

Farms, logging, campgrounds, parks, condominiums, summer houses, and shopping malls—human beings try to use the land in multiple ways, but we are discovering that there is not always enough open space to go around. As increasing numbers of people with different goals and ambitions crowd together in the same places, conflict seems inevitable.

I've seen a man from New York City point to a cow and ask, sincerely, "Is that a goat?"

A second man, also from the city, questioned the authenticity of Howe Caverns, a vast network of caves spread under several miles of farmland near Albany: "Were these caves once in Rochester?"

The buffoons in these stories are nearly always New Yorkers. Sometimes, rarely, they are from Connecticut or New Jersey— mere extensions of the big city, jokes in themselves. The tellers of these stories are always from upstate—rural, cow country—where there is open scorn for the city and a deep suspicion of the urban way of life.

There is a proposal—treated as a joke, alas, because it wouldn't stand up to a vote—to give the city to New Jersey and declare the rest of the state West Vermont. People who must crawl out of bed at four every morning and stagger bleary eyed across a cold floor to milk the cows naturally resent people who don't have to—all the more so if the city folk think milk is made in the back room of a grocery store.

Food in the city comes conveniently presliced, wrapped in plastic, packaged in cardboard boxes. But the rural family sitting down to a dinner of lamb chops may have personally fed the sheep and sent them to the slaughter. Perhaps their freezers are stocked with venison or moose that they hunted themselves.

Rural peoples share a penchant for hunting. It's a pleasant autumn ritual to suit up in orange and stalk deer through the woods— a chance to pad softly on the fallen leaves, to sift quietly through the trees, human versus animal. Hunting heightens the senses of sight, sound, smell. It's a chance to play in the outdoors, a vacation that begins the moment you set foot in the woods and ends when you return to your farm. I know a heavyset lazy man who spends his summer mornings sunk in the comfort of an armchair, sipping milky brown coffee. Autumn comes, and only then does he spring to life, rising early to greet the cool dawn. "I've gone hunting every year for the past ten years and gotten nothing," he says. "It's my chance to get outdoors, walk around. But if I get a chance, I shoot." Typically, it is the men who hunt, occasionally joined by a few bold women.

Is there a right to hunt? From Maine to Georgia in every stretch of woods, hunting season sends out orange-jacketed teenagers, adults, and old men to stalk through the brush with guns. Is it necessary in this age of supermarkets and fast food? Distant explosions start at dawn and continue all day. People grow accustomed to the noise and learn not to listen for it, the way houses near airports can tremble furiously underneath the wake of jet planes, unnoticed by their inhabitants; the way the patter of rain on leaves, to those who are used to it, is a soothing sound, not an irritant. Familiarity plugs our ears with soft cotton.

In a restaurant near Paradox, New York, twelve miles west of historic Ticonderoga, a woman made the claim that her town was founded by an M.D. and a D.D.S., a pair of "docs."

I admired the pun enough to linger over lunch, just to hear any other witticisms she chanced to tell. Writers do this; we eavesdrop. The woman sat in the next booth, talking to her wrinkle-faced friend, a local. She began to spin a tale about a man who drove up from New York to hunt deer. He was wearing a bright orange vest with a red checkered cap, and from a distance he almost looked like a real outdoorsman. Up close you could tell he was from the city. For one thing, he snapped twigs underfoot and let branches scrape across his vest, making enough noise to scare away any deer within a mile. And, by one account, when he saw fellow hunters, he shouted hello. All day, he stalked through the woods, usually in old, thickly wooded areas with no growth on the ground, where there weren't any deer. By chance, around five o'clock, he saw an animal that hadn't fled after the racket he made stomping through the brush. He shot it, strapped his prize on the top of his station wagon, and drove off into the sunset.

The animal was, in fact, a St. Bernard. The man was arrested while celebrating his "first deer" at a bar, the dead dog still on top of his car.

"This one is true and sad," insists the storyteller, laughing. She removes her glasses, wipes her eyes. Her son, she claims, saw the man in the woods shortly before he killed the dog. He hollered a hello.

I first heard the St. Bernard story third hand, from a nonhunter down in Albany; it may not be true. Somehow this little folktale has migrated all the way from Albany to Ticonderoga with barely any change. The moral is obvious and cruel: City folk are fools who should not be let loose in the woods with a gun. (Down in the less-safe areas of New York City, perhaps they joke about naive farmers who should not be let loose on the streets *without* a gun.)

It's not their fault if city folk have such ignorance that they mistake a dog for a deer. They live in a society cut off from wilderness and from agriculture. But it is their fault if despite such ignorance they're willing to kill anything that moves in the woods. This produces a tension between local hunters, who claim to know what they are doing, and "summer folk"—back in the woods in autumn—who obviously do not.

An opposing view is that all hunters are fools and should not be loose in the woods. That is the opinion of animal-rights activists, the groups that stalk hunters with horns, stereos, and drums to frighten away deer. Such a view is rigorously opposed in Maine, in the Adirondacks, and anywhere rural. "I respect their right to an opinion," says an outdoorsman, "and I'm not a gun nut or a member of the NRA, but I don't want anyone telling me I can't hunt."

Certainly, true hunters want no fools with guns in their woods. The problem is that no one considers himself a fool. In 1988 a woman named Karen Wood, newly moved to Maine from Iowa with her husband and two babies, went out into her backyard in November, supposedly to tell a hunter he was too close to the house. She was wearing white gloves, dark clothes. It was a short walk, a hundred feet or so from her back door. White gloves look, it is said, like the tail of a deer.

The hunter said later he saw something white dash through the trees and thought it was a "flag," a deer's tail. He shot at it—an accident. When he ran up to look over his prize, what he found was a dead woman. The children lost their mother. The man's explanation was generally accepted, though a few older hunters ridiculed it. "What idiot would shoot a deer in the ass!" I heard another hunter say with a snort.

The incident has already entered popular culture as a folktale. Some retellings have Karen Wood go out back to hang laundry. Some omit the white gloves or say that the hunter was drunk.

In Maine there was much sympathy for the victim and for the children, and also sympathy for the hunter, Donald Rogerson. But the hunter escaped all punishment save the burden of his conscience, and because of that verdict there was widespread opinion outside of Maine that people there felt no sympathy at all for the victim, that the citizens of Maine regarded her as a transplanted Down Easter, really just an Iowa vacationer who didn't know how to live in the North Woods. She was careless; it was her fault. Mr. Rogerson's supporters inflamed this opinion, perhaps inadvertently, by implying exactly that, by suggesting that his conscience would and should go easy on him for exactly those reasons. He said he was sorry—very sorry—but in no way neglectful.

"You can't have these people just walking out in the woods like that," said an acquaintance of mine, echoing the sentiments of many Mainers. "She didn't know what she was doing. She should have been wearing orange."

No one knows why Karen Wood walked outside at just that moment, but she probably did not know the hunter was there. She didn't call out or warn the hunter in any way. She was wearing white gloves and dark clothes, but it was a game warden, not the hunter, who first suggested that white gloves might have resembled the tail of a deer. The hunter was sixty-three yards away, and his truck was parked nearby. He said he didn't know he was so close to houses. Two shots were fired—one hit and killed Karen Wood. An editorial in the *Bangor Daily News* blamed the tragedy on "the development of what were traditionally wilderness areas and the influx of large numbers of people who do not share or understand the traditional views and values of native Mainers."

Donald Rogerson is said to have felt tremendous guilt and will never hunt again. Had his defenders shown a little more sympathy for Karen Wood, rather than blaming the victim for her ignorance of local customs, the event might have been viewed as a tragedy all around, rather than as a miscarriage of justice. No one—except, perhaps, Rogerson—planned to stop hunting because of it. No one looked down on hunters because of it. It is accepted; accidents happen. They shouldn't, but they do. By all accounts, it was a matter of recklessness. Exactly who was the reckless party is still disputed.

Years earlier I heard of a similar tragedy, closer to Katahdin country, perhaps an even better illustration of the philosophy of Maine hunters. The killer was a boy, only fourteen; the victim, a longtime resident of Maine, a man in his fifties, a fellow hunter. For some unknown reason, he was wearing green. It was out in the deep woods, far from any town. The boy shot him, discovered his mistake, and was sick for days. A local man criticized the deceased. "I have no sympathy at all for that fool who was killed. He's better off dead. Look what this boy must live with for the rest of his life. He now refuses to touch a gun, turns green at the sound of one, and will never hunt again."

Thoreau was not a hunter, but he saw his neighbors often with guns in hand. "There are so many sportsmen out that the ducks have no rest on the Great Meadows," he wrote in 1858. "They sit uneasy on the water, looking about, without feeding, and I see one man endeavor to approach a flock crouchingly through the meadow for half a mile, with india-rubber boots on, where the water is often a foot deep. This has been going on, on these meadows, ever since the town was settled, and will go on as long as ducks settle here."

There do exist reputable hunters who recognize the effects of predation and respect the sacrifice made by their prey. Some seek the thrill of the chase, the scent of autumn in the woods; to enjoy these things, it isn't necessary to blast a dart of hot metal through a deer's guts. Some know this; they hold back at the fatal instant, choose not to fire. Some must hunt for food.

There are also sport hunters who play a game with guns, who like to decorate their walls with what they kill. Their quest is to affix the animal's head to their living-room wall, to sever neck from torso and send a chunk of deer or moose to a taxidermist, who takes out eyes that once saw and replaces them with dead glass balls. Lazy ones just leave the bodies where they fall, a small contribution to the soil.

Of course, no one looks into a mirror and sees such a ruthless savage. One deer per person, goes the argument, is not a threat to the environment, nor a sign of blood lust. It's a sign of being hungry—every man has a commitment to stock a deer in his family's freezer.

Hunting is also a ritual necessary to manage the wildlife population, to prevent mass starvation of deer in the winter. That it happens to be a pleasurable experience is a happy coincidence.

A counter argument attacks the necessity of hunting. That death, suffering, and predation exist in nature is a fact that cannot be denied. But that does not mean modern human hunting is modeled after nature. When herds of caribou and deer roamed over Katahdin's tablelands, wolves preyed on the weak and injured, the ones least likely to survive. Every kill left more food for the strong, who survived to pass on their genes. But humans tend to go after the strong, the animals most likely to live through a winter of starvation. We keep score, counting the points—the bigger the better. Clearly, the best way for a deer to survive hunting season is to be small and weak, lacking antlers.

"I could go into the woods with a club and come out with a doe," says my friend. He does not shoot does or fawns, or anything pitiful. Most years, he does not kill anything at all. But sighting a large buck with fourteen points, one that would surely get his picture in the local paper, there comes a distant explosion in the woods.

The question of how best to use our open spaces and natural resources is a volatile one. Wildlife preserve or hunting grounds? Virgin forest or clear cut? Untouched splendor or oil wells? In a democracy, these are weighty matters. And as our population grows, the schism between rural and urban opinion only widens. As Bangor native Michael Foster told a *New York Times* reporter in 1990, "The problem is that your dyed-in-the-wool hunters just believe they have an inalienable right to hunt everywhere. Local, indigenous native Mainers are slightly provincial anyway. To have outside people come in and shape policy, they really resent that."

Each flip of a switch in a ballot box makes a quiet clicking sound, a noise muffled by the curtain that wraps our vote in privacy. But each vote has the power to fire up a chainsaw a hundred miles away and make the wood of a white pine scream and snap as it tumbles to the soil. "The civilized man regards the pine tree as his enemy," wrote Thoreau. "He will fell it and let in the light, grub it up and raise wheat or rye there. It is no better than a fungus to him." Many share that opinion today. Many, but not all.

A vote can also plant a tree. In 1990 voters in New York State for the first time faced a proposal to set aside two billion dollars for the purchase of private lands in the Adirondack Park and elsewhere. Voters slipped behind the black fabric of the ballot booth, pulled the curtain shut, and thought hard.

The proposal was championed by then-Governor Mario Cuomo, a liberal Democrat more or less detested by the generally conservative voters of the rural north country. But the big city loved him. As a general rule of thumb, urban dwellers vote green; ruralites by contrast choose industry, development, progress. Inhabitants of the suburbs split the difference. "The grass is always greener."

If only city dwellers had voted, the park proposal would have passed by an overwhelming margin. The environmental bond enthralled millions of urban New Yorkers who had never set foot on Mount Marcy or run a curious thumb down the white stripe of glacial striations. They had never felt the cool strokes of alpine winds or noticed the prisms of autumn leaves—but perhaps they still hoped to someday.

Perhaps it's best if some people never do experience the mountains; that will permit them to keep their ideals. As my friend Sarah, a native New Yorker, once remarked, "I like the outdoors in theory, but in practice we don't get along."

James Watt, an avid proponent of hydroelectric dams, once rafted down the Colorado River and found it "boring"—much to the dismay of environmentalists. They had hoped such a scenic and playful trip would change his mind. Instead, that trip merely eliminated any lingering doubts he may have had that the Glen Canyon Dam had been the best choice for that area.

How many millions of New Yorkers must have lingering doubts

about locking up the Adirondacks for bear and deer? How many Americans still must question the need for an untainted Alaskan wilderness at the expense of wood and oil? Do we really need it all?

Upstate, in counties near the Adirondack Park, it was nearly impossible to find someone who had voted yes for the environmental bond. Members of the John Birch Society, who do not like trees, naturally opposed it. "It's a land grab," they said. "A plot by the government to take land out of private hands."

Most people in upstate New York had more pressing concerns; they feared their downstate neighbors more than communists or feds. "We don't want city folk here in our woods messing with it. They don't know what it's like to live here." The speaker is a small, elderly man, five feet tall plus a few inches. His face is deeply lined, yellowed and spotted, but his eyes are alive, focused. He runs a general store near Lake Placid, so he sees a fair share of tourists. Fastened to the wall behind the counter is an old musket.

"No one cares about us up here," he says. It's the governor he's talking to.

In the green hills where I lived at the time, the votes ran six to one against the purchase proposal. All nearby counties—Fulton, Montgomery, and Hamilton—had the same margin, or greater. In the end, this sizable advantage—measured against the massive 75 percent approval of New York City—made the measure fail by a slim margin.

I voted yes, knowing that the answer would be no. My vote was doomed to fail. Had it stood any chance of success, I might have thought twice, for then I would have had to consider its impact on the region and the people, my neighbors. In the same state of mind, I once voted for a neighbor whose politics are the antithesis of my own, simply because he could not possibly win. It was a message of sympathy, a cheer for the hometown—and he lost, thank goodness, two votes to one.

Maine is already facing similar opportunities. "All we ever do here is ski and wait for the next referendum," a native woman tells me. The voting booth is open, but out in the woods the chainsaws and condominium developers are waiting. Environmentalists hope to protect millions of acres of forest, surrounding the mountains and forest core like a shield, to prevent abuses by corporations like Georgia-Pacific, and to keep the tourist-trap entrepreneurs out of business. They fear that the road to Katahdin, a path through birches, pines, and hissing streams, could quickly fill with motels, restaurants, and amusement parks, like the neon slum of Ellsworth, which precedes Bar Harbor.

Should protected wilderness areas expand by several million acres, as one proposal suggests, there will be no jobs left in towns like Millinocket, Medway, Patten, or Mattawamkeag. Soon, these towns would not exist at all. So far, the white bark of birch trees still grins at the mountain like giant teeth in the sun. But environmentalists are no longer smiling.

How ironic—and sad—that the economy requires us both to preserve and profit from wilderness. To a paper company, a hardwood tree is a weed; their forests are not natural. The paper companies do replant, it's true, for their goal is to tame our forests, not eradicate them. But they replant softwoods only. The colors of autumn are lost on a tree farm. A blossom is alien. More importantly, underneath those millions of rows of needles and cones there are no wild blueberries to munch, no shrubs and thistles where rabbits can hide from predators, no low branches for grazing deer. When the growth is gone, will the wildlife move on?

For now, animals in the woods of Maine seem friendly, even careless or unwary. Bob Howes, a ranger, talks about a tourist who slept on the ground outside his lean-to one warm summer night and was hugged by a bear. The very spot he had chosen to sleep on smelled of pancake batter, where someone had happened to spill a bowl. The man awoke around midnight to feel a hairy paw groping his shoulder, trying to roll him out of the way. Predictably, the man screamed; so did the bear. Seconds later, both man and bear fled in terror, fortunately in opposite directions.

Moose are the most suspicious animals. They keep an eye out for people, but don't mind if folk sit quietly on a rock and watch them yank plants off the bottoms of ponds. Moose seek out the campgrounds and spend nights on the lawns. At Kidney Pond, rangers put a salt lick at the edge of a clearing to lure animals out of the woods. Moose who take the bait quickly get used to the cameras and the people—and given time, the people get used to moose as well.

The first time I saw a moose step out of the woods near a campground, she was cautiously surrounded by humans, the object of a dozen pictures. Children crawled on their bellies in the grass, as close as they dared, inching forward on their elbows. The moose licked salt, looked up. A red-haired boy with a camera had crawled too close. I expected the moose to flee or charge. Instead, she took a bold step forward, sniffing—and the alarmed photographer bolted and ran. Curiosity, it seems, is not limited to human beings.

Of course, the moose's appeal soon faded. For a day, then two, the moose stayed in a clearing near the salt lick. Few campers cared; the moose was just one more boulder among the trees, covered with hair. They started pointing their cameras at other things—trees, the pond, the mountains. Occasionally at night, a sleepy camper would wander back from a trip to the outhouse and complain about tripping over that "goddam moose"—an exaggeration; you don't trip over a moose, you walk into it, like a wall.

On day three, the guest moose (or host moose, as she surely considered herself) encountered a surge of popularity when she brought back a calf. Children gathered round, the cameras came out again. Click, click, click—the sound of tourists in the woods. Soon the young moose trembled on weak, stick-like legs. He stuck close to mama.

Two days later the novelty wore off—again. Mama moose, trying to make friends, strode out of Kidney Pond toward a group of men throwing horseshoes. She stood between the rings, dripping fat drops of pond water on the grass. Unfortunately, she interrupted the game. They shouted, "Go on, git!" "Hi! Get out of there, you!" The men waved and jumped up and down. The moose opened her eyes wide; she fled. Then the men resumed throwing horseshoes. One man scored a ringer; I heard it clang.

One afternoon while I was driving toward a quiet corner of the mountains, my car startled a bull moose. He began to jog away, drifting from right to left, searching for a way off the road. I followed at five miles per hour, expecting him to disappear into the dense shrubs and trees alongside the Nesowadnehunk tote road. But he didn't flee. Granite boulders rose steeply on either side, clothed in moss and ferns. The roots of saplings gripped the rocks. A wall. The moose sauntered away. I thought he must surely be terrified, but he didn't look worried at all—he just loped down the road with the stride of a giant, waiting for a place to escape. Then the rocks dropped away. He was gone.

Bicycles and Bagpipes

In *Walden*, Thoreau mocks a farm boy sent to work alone in some distant field in Massachusetts, who later returned ill from that silent, open space. He was haunted by the lack of human presence. "He had never seen such a dull and out-of-the-way place," writes Thoreau. "The folks were all gone off; why, you couldn't even hear the whistle!"

When Thoreau himself traipsed into the wilderness, he seldom went far. As a blistering 1908 review of his work in the *Atlantic Monthly* notes, "Woodcraft is not a profession which can be picked up by browsing in Massachusetts pastures."

The cottage Thoreau inhabited for two years at the edge of Walden Pond stood little more than a stone's throw from the Fitchburg Railroad. Each day a train's whistle pierced the air, briefly silencing the chatter of jays in the trees. Thoreau no doubt paused in his labors and leaned on his hoe in the bean field, listening to the echoes subside. At times, it was a reassuring sound, or at least a comfortably familiar one. The steam engine, belching smoke and noise, was inescapable. Many times Thoreau crossed back and forth over the cinder tracks while walking to town to gossip at the post office or have dinner with the Emersons. Once, he even hopped aboard the train and rode its rails east on his way to a lonely mountain in Maine.

Wherever he went, he saw or heard the engines of human progress. "It requires considerable skill in crossing a country to avoid the houses and too cultivated parts," he wrote in his journal in 1852. He used hills and trees as a screen in order to "pass the enemy's lines where houses are thick." To create the illusion of solitude, he said, one must "shut every window with an apple tree."

Centuries earlier, in stark contrast, the trees were the enemy. The woods were truly wild, even dangerous. A lone human was vulnerable prey for mountain lions, bears, and wolves. A solitary walk through the trees then was a form of exile or even suicide—a sudden (and often permanent) amputation of the bond between family and friends. No roads or rails existed to carry home the lost and weary. The forest, far from offering a spiritual escape, actually frightened the first Europeans to set eyes on the New World. They stood aghast, offended by nature. Snakes, devils, and worse lurked in those deep, leafy shadows. A treacherous twilight surrounded their tiny human settlements by the sea.

Today, of course, it is the wilderness that exists in shrunken pockets, bordered on all sides by civilization, suburbs, airports, multilane highways. Predictably, our attitudes toward the natural world have gone topsy-turvy. We now seek out nature and revel in it, though, like Thoreau, we can never quite escape our growing numbers. "You can walk in the woods in no direction but you hear the sound of the axe," Thoreau wrote. Today, there is nowhere you can go without hearing the train whistle or the rumble of trucks and cars.

This afternoon, in that same woodsy corner of New England where Thoreau once "travelled widely," I have set out to explore the thin slice of wilderness that remains. "Explore" may be too strong a word; I will never leave paved roads. The moment I set out I hear the faint hum of a commercial jet airliner, far overhead. Looking up, I see the white contrails merge with cirrus clouds. Lower down, sunlight glints off the glass windows of newly built houses. I move, and one window disappears behind a tree trunk, but there are not enough apple trees here to "shut" them all.

For most Americans an expedition into nature involves seeing little more than a glimpse of a rare owl in their backyard, or a crow's nest squirreled away behind a neon sign at the shopping mall. If we're lucky, we might catch a glimpse of deer in the fields as we whisk past in our cars.

I've decided to slow the pace a bit. Even now, my bicycle slides across the blacktop as smoothly as a puck on ice; gravity has forgotten me. As I ride out of the shadows on little Station Road and pedal across U.S. Route 9, the temperature jumps a degree or two— a small but remarkable difference. Trapped under a roof of maple leaves, the chillier breezes of morning linger on back roads all day long, while the naked sun and the fumes of cars blast Route 9 with the intense heat of summer.

I wait for a gap in the line of traffic, then kick back at the gravel, gliding across the road. A horn honks. Briefly, the grumbles of the wind are drowned by whining engines. This roar of traffic rises sharply in pitch to the south, then sinks into a growl as cars, pickup trucks, and semis streak past me—a classic example of the Doppler effect. Quickly, I click up a gear and reenter the quiet, shady forest on the other side. The road narrows to a dimly lit tunnel of trees.

A bicyclist—or a pedestrian—can see things that drivers miss, like an inch-deep crack in the street, or a pocket of hot air at an intersection, or that speed trap lurking just around the corner. Lately I have noticed something else, too. Millions of us with hectic schedules pass daily from house to car to office and seldom see the outdoors. On muggy summer days we quickly step from air-conditioned cars into air-conditioned offices with only a momentary passage through the uncomfortable heat in between. I confess

I am as guilty as the rest. Strangely enough, that's why I choose to ride a bicycle up, over, and around the hills every day. I commute.

Though traveling by bicycle saves gas and wins a nod of approval from the environmentalists, my reasons are purely selfish. I miss the outdoors.

Something about the outdoors draws us, whether we're looking for inspiration or seeking to "find ourselves" or merely trying to keep fit. People respond to this urge in varying degrees: going on a picnic, riding a bicycle, hunting on an autumn morning, climbing a mountain. In extreme cases, they may even set aside five months to walk the Appalachian Trail from Georgia to Maine.

For my own peace of mind I began one year to ride my bicycle to work and to the grocery store, observing nature along the way. Since I lived six miles out of town, the daily ride was not exercise per se, just a chore that needed doing. An enjoyable chore, it turned out. My car was put out to pasture; weeds sprouted around the tires.

Quickly I learned to endure the hills with a gallon of milk, a bag of apples, and a loaf of bread on my back. I even explored new routes through the low-hanging trees. Who needs a car?

Then, alas, it rained.

I succumbed to the occasional use of an Oldsmobile. But if it merely drizzled, with tiny droplets floating in the air like a soupy fog, I put on an oversized blue parka, draped it over my pack, and donned a ridiculous pair of yellow rain pants. I looked silly, stayed dry, and still enjoyed the outdoors.

Today, sweating under the hot sun, I have sought shady back roads as an alternative to busy Route 9. There's no hurry. As I ride along, kernels of weathered gray pavement crunch under my tires. The ground is a blur.

Breezes mutter wordless phrases in the leaves. A squirrel, startled by the swift, silent appearance of my bicycle, drops his acorns at the side of the road and hops—panicked—onto a maple tree. He pauses halfway up the trunk and watches me with tiny black eyes.

Up, up, up. I stand and grind my way up the hill, swerving into the center of the road. The pedals no longer turn smoothly, but stop and start, crank and grind. My legs must work each step, like a hiker stuck on a steep stretch of mountain.

This afternoon I've forgotten which way is home. Quite deliberately, I am lost. At the top of the hill the road levels off, becoming an easy, pleasant ride. A soft breeze pushes against my back like a strong, invisible hand; I feel like I could coast uphill. Soon the branches spread apart over the road, opening again for the sun.

Summer heat dissolves the breeze, and the push at my back falters; I must pedal. On a wide, empty stretch of road ahead, there is a dark shimmer like a pool of water—a common mirage. It soon fades.

That mirage, like the Doppler shift of car engines on Route 9, belongs in the realm of physics. What looks like water is just a reflection of the sky, bounced toward our eyes by a thin layer of warm air above the asphalt. The physicist Ernest Rutherford once remarked that everything is divided into two categories: "physics and stamp collecting." So cycling, too, I suppose is a branch of physics, unless you happen to be riding to the post office.

A magazine once printed a survey of what bikers think about while riding. Sex topped the list; contemplation of physics wasn't even mentioned. Professional athletes and commuters, it seems, have different things on their minds.

I am nearly home when the sun dodges behind a cloud, throwing shadows over the trees. For a time, I just pedal once and glide, pedal and glide, resting after the mile-and-a-half climb. Then in the distance, I hear . . . bagpipes? The strains of music drift closer.

There is a clearing not far ahead, where strong wind skims across a pond, kicking up tiny waves. On the crest of each inch-high ripple gleams a golden flicker of sunlight; a million tiny suns dance on the water. This natural phenomenon does not normally produce bagpipe music. What is going on here?

The lake sweeps around the road on both sides. Bullfrogs clear their throats in the tall grass along the shore. A man sits there with his back against a tree, his eyes hidden in the shade of a Red Sox cap. He is throwing clumps of sandwich to some ducks who have waddled away from the pond in search of tastier food. The ducks shuffle comically on their feet in front of the man, their eyes focused on the scrap of bread in his hand. He tosses it, and the flock scurries back to snatch it off the ground. They quack for more, but the shriek of bagpipes overwhelms them.

On a hill above the pond stands a tall, brown-haired man in a kilt, piping the strains of a highland bagpipe waltz, "Skye Boat." I recognize the tune. Far from southern New England, I have ridden, quite unexpectedly, straight to the hills of Scotland. What happened, I wonder, to the ocean on the way? Is this Brigadoon, come alive for a day?

I know it's easier to tap a gas pedal in a car than to pedal up a hill. And perhaps, if I wanted to exercise merely for the sake of exercise (a thing unheard of in Thoreau's era; it's hard to imagine Thoreau or Emerson running on treadmills in a gym in Concord) a stationary bicycle would be more convenient. But this is what we miss—the wind, the trees, the unexpected. No indoor fitness regimen has ever provided ducks, bagpipes, and the woods of New England to supplement push-ups and sit-ups. For now, so long as I must suffer to stay in shape, this is how I prefer to pay the piper.

A Tale of Two Mountains

Thoreau had a terrible habit of starting fires. One April day he and a friend paddled a boat down the Concord River, intending to fish for food and then camp overnight on the river's banks. The river was low; the ground dry. Thoreau's small cooking fire ignited the grass and spread. A frantic attempt to stomp the flames out with hands and feet failed, and the fire leapt from grasses to bushes, bushes to trees. The path of the inferno led directly toward Concord village. "That way went the flames with wild delight, and we felt that we had no control over the demonic creature to which we had given birth."

Thoreau ran two miles to warn the town, and a church bell rang, summoning citizens to battle the blaze. Dozens gathered with hoes and shovels. Thoreau stood among them. He alone was not panicked or fearful. "I have set fire to the forest, but I have done no wrong therein, and now it is as if the lightning had done it," Thoreau wrote in his journal. "These flames are but consuming their natural food." Natural forest fires were common and, in Thoreau's opinion, beneficial, as long as they did not spread too far. Such fires "will clean the forest floor like a broom perfectly smooth and clear, —no twigs left to crackle underfoot, the dead and rotten wood removed." Huckleberries and blueberry bushes thrived in areas cleared by fire, and abundant fruits enticed birds and wild animals in great numbers. "It is inspiriting to walk amid the fresh green sprouts of grass and shrubbery pushing upward through the charred surface with more vigorous growth."

At least a hundred acres of wood burned that day, to the chagrin of the lot's owners, but to the delight of Thoreau. He wrote, "That night I watched the fire, where some stumps still flamed at midnight in the midst of the blackened waste, wandering through the woods by myself." He made his way back to the source of the first spark, his campfire, and discovered his fish dinner "now broiled," lying on the burnt grass.

I mention this anecdote only because, a few years later, Thoreau almost burned down Mount Washington.

Mount Washington, New Hampshire, is one of the high points along the Appalachian Trail. It's impossible to see Katahdin from atop the 6,288-foot-high mountain, but the Maine state line is just a few miles to the east. For thru-hikers who reach this point, the end of the trail is near—and yet far. The last 280 miles are perhaps the most difficult. Hikers on the final leg of the journey are usually on their last legs themselves. "There are people who drop out even up here," says thru-hiker Richard Bailey. They give up, he says, "even though they're doing fine, physically. After you've hiked 1,850 miles you're just psychologically drained and tired."

Thoreau wrote passionately and at length—over a hundred pages—about his journey to Katahdin. But he recorded little about his two trips to Mount Washington in 1839 and 1858. Perhaps that was just as well. One of Thoreau's companions kindled a camp-fire near some dry moss and accidentally set fire to the whole of Tuckerman Ravine, Mount Washington's largest glacial cirque. Thoreau described in his journal the flames "spreading off with great violence and crackling over the mountain, and making us jump for our baggage." He noted that it "spread particularly fast in the pro-cumbent creeping spruce." A paragraph later he and his friends had traveled on, documenting shrubs and flowers lower down the mountain, leaving the forest fire to rage behind them unobserved. How times have changed. A careless camper today would face heavy fines for such a violation. "The Forest Service would not look kindly on it," a ranger tells me with wry understatement. "They'd be in big trouble."

Significant change occurred to Mount Washington even in the nineteen years after Thoreau's first visit. In 1839 the mountaintop was still barren, wild, untamed. By 1858 two buildings had been constructed on the summit, accommodating hikers with drinks and a roof over their heads. Growing numbers of people already were starting to visit the mountains for no other purpose than to admire the view.

The only peak I have hiked as often as Katahdin is Mount Washington, where for seven years I worked as a weather watcher at the observatory on its summit.

Usually I drove to work. Some days, feeling energetic, I com-muted on my feet. I once discovered a crevice where silvery sheets of mica jutted up from the quartzite base. I rubbed a thumb across thin pages of mica, flipping through a story at least three hundred million years old. Then the shadow of a cloud fell upon me; I shiv-ered, dropped the rock back into the crack where it had lain un-disturbed for eons, and hurried up the trail until my body heat warmed me again.

What I found on the summit was changed from what Thoreau

had seen—different, too, from I was used to seeing on Katahdin. Mounts Washington and Katahdin represent two radically different approaches to enjoying the wilderness. Katahdin is regulated, restricted, "forever wild." Its summit can be reached only on foot. An auto road and railway lead up to the summit of Mount Washington, and the architecture of the observatory, the visitors' center, and the radio transmitters is taller than the natural peak. While hiking up Mount Washington, my eyes are drawn not to the summit itself but the looming metal transmitting tower of WHOM-FM.

I remember Thoreau's desire to look *at* a mountain, not off it. He wasn't kidding. On Katahdin, you must strain with sweaty arms to lift yourself across the rough granite inch by inch, pebble by pebble. You have no choice but to stare the mountain in the face. In the end, the view at the top is a crisp reward for many hours of toil.

Mount Washington's summit also peers off a stony platform into the distance, but the panorama there pleases us in a half-satisfying way. Perhaps it is too easy to get here. We haven't earned our view. It is too tempting to drive up the road, powered by gasoline, letting the climatic lines that divide the worlds of evergreens and maple trees whisk by in a whir. We have reached our destination, but no journey has been taken. Instead, we arrive at the summit with all the ease of flipping open a picture book. The asphalt surface of a road winds back down the slopes toward civilization.

Outside, the winds may rage with hurricane force, but from inside the buildings on Mount Washington's summit, the tea-kettle whine of the wind is just a whisper. In summer, the wind's howl subsides to a soft murmur, and the mountain sits under our feet like a horse that won't buck. The challenge is gone. We have, we think, tamed the mountain.

Only in fog, when boulders and buildings are hidden, do I ever forget the difference between the two mountains.

Fog veils the ground this morning, so it is difficult to see. Halfway up the trail, I trip over a gnarled black root. It coiled around my ankle, yanking me down. I dig two fistfuls of mud, pushing myself off the ground. As I brush away the soil on my jeans, the roots slink back into the mist.

The shadows of tall trees stand like sentinels on both sides of the trail. I pull higher, higher up the mountain, and the trees start to shrink until they are gone. Boulders soon materialize. I step through boulder fields, each stone floating in the fog like an asteroid in ether. "I looked with awe at the ground I trod on," Thoreau once wrote, and now I can sympathize. Thoreau remarked, "We have not seen pure Nature, unless we have seen her thus vast, and drear, and inhuman."

Up, up. I stumble past rocks and thorny shrubs, traveling deeper into the heart of a cloud. No landmarks or signs point the way. I could be anywhere.

For a while the sun shines, but then it starts to dim, shrink, fade. I feel as if I am sinking, falling ever farther from the sun. Fog swirls and eddies overhead. The liquid mist pushes me down, even as I struggle to climb higher. I am drowning. Fog washes against my face like ocean spray. Like a rock I plummet. The last glint of the sun—a buoy now floating far, far overhead—disappears.

Thoreau, in one of his most imaginative moments, called this mountaintop the rubble of a world not yet born. I agree. At my feet, boulders sit in bricks and slabs like God's building blocks, waiting to be stacked to some unknown purpose. The mist conceals all else.

In fog, time stops. There is nothing to measure time by, nothing to see, nothing to measure. The past lies twenty paces behind me. The future is a gray haze into which I must walk and disappear. Ten paces ahead lies the horizon, the edge of time. I struggle up, walking from boulder to boulder. No sun exists anymore, just a dull glimmer like twilight. I shiver and pull my jacket tighter against my skin.

A mosquito buzzes out of nowhere and whines past my ear. Then it is gone. I'm alone again. Even the wind stills.

The fog constricts. I wonder now whether I am a giant or a dwarf. How can I tell? There is no solid matter to compare myself to. Am I lost? What if I emerge from this fog on some other mountain, in some other time?

I no longer remember where I started. Mount Washington? Have I walked so far through the mist that Katahdin's granite now rolls underfoot? Perhaps I will know when I climb to the end of the trail at last and poke my head through the top of the cloud. But no shrub or stone or sign is visible in the mist to help me identify one peak or the next. Whether this is Katahdin or Washington or neither, I cannot tell the difference and do not care. Until I choose to climb back down, to return to the land below the clouds where the wind is a gentle breeze, the name of this mountain means nothing.

"The question is not where did the traveller go? what places did he see?" Thoreau wrote, "but who was the traveller? how did he travel? how genuine an experience did he get?" Thoreau would understand. He has been here before me.

Forever Wild

On a mountaintop I stood alone, a solitary witness to the dissolution of the earth. Gusts of wind hurled clouds across the sky—clouds that dipped down and washed across the boulder fields on their way east to the Atlantic Ocean. A white speck of sun burned through the haze for a time, but the clouds thickened and then it was gone. In the distance, far below me, the smokestacks of Millinocket coughed up tiny plumes of smog. Soon the town vanished.

Entire forests were erased, their trees plucked one by one from the landscape. To the north, little Traveler Mountain faded like the slag of a sand castle, swallowed by the sea. The ocean of fog drowned the green Wassataquoik Valley. Waves of fog crashed against the bald North Peaks, and what was once solid matter—granite and rhyolite—liquefied and dissolved in an instant.

I lost the world on a crag a mile below the summit, on the Appalachian Trail. Soon only a tiny stepping-stone of rock survived at my feet. I reached out an arm, a probe, but my fingertips vanished, lopped off at the edge of vision. Worried, I yanked my hand back. I wondered what would happen if I stepped forward into that swirling netherworld. All that remained of planet Earth was this tiny circle of tundra set afloat in the clouds.

Outside the gray walls the wind was screaming. My wristwatch said two o'clock in the afternoon, but did time matter? Was the earth still down there, somewhere? I remembered that the place where I stood was more than four thousand feet high, and a view of half of Maine once extended behind me. I recalled drinking from a cold, clear stream two miles back, under tall spruce trees, then scrambling over boulders, splitting open my boots on sharp rocks. The evidence suggests a world once existed here, but now it was gone. To step into those walls of mist was to plunge into the ether forever.

Of course, the open circle moved with me when I walked away. I never fell off or came to the edge of the world. An hour later the cloud slid off the mountaintop and sunshine returned, and the thousand lakes of the state of Maine reappeared on the horizon as if painted on a gray canvas. In all that time I met no one. Solitude was my reason for climbing a mountain that day.

Back in 1852 the Reverend John Todd, one of the first of the new wave of recreational climbers, said, "Your first feeling is, you want to be and must be alone." Todd and a friend toiled up the steep Keep Ridge, guided by a Native American, to Pamola and Baxter peaks. Near the end, Todd quickened his pace and left his companions far down the trail. "When I reached the summit, my companion and guide were more than half a mile off, and right glad I was. I did not want to see or hear any thing human."

Thoreau, too, ascended alone into the clouds, while his cousin and his friends, who had no literary aspirations, set up camp. He waded across streams, bushwhacked through shrubs and stunted trees, and at last clawed his way up the spine of granite-strewn Mount Katahdin. Pebbles and loose stones ricocheted down the slopes, kicked loose by his feet. Each stride took him ever farther from the teeming life of the lowlands. The desolation of the alpine windswept tundra brought to his mind epic mythology and the creation of earth. Thoreau felt he'd passed back in time. He invoked Prometheus the fire bringer and imagined the formation of the earth as a rain of rocks from the sky. "The tops of mountains are among the unfinished parts of the globe, whither it is a slight insult to the gods to climb and pry into their secrets."

Had he brought along his friends for company, his writing in *Ktaadn* might have set a less humble tone. A shared experience would have been less frightful—but also, perhaps, less inspiring.

I knew the mountain would change while hidden in clouds. Things invisible to the eye would move; it had happened before on a distant ridge, where the unexpected jostling of two large rocks shook the earth like the footsteps of Pamola. Most transformations are more subtle. Wind pushes grains of sand. Stems of alpine sedges tussle in the breeze and rearrange themselves. Puddles of water evaporate off the rocks. I expected these changes. What I did not expect was to see, just ahead, thirty human beings appear out of the thinning mist, all in a cluster.

They must have climbed up a separate trail, perhaps following the old route of surveyor Charles Jackson to the summit. A second group hiked behind me. I soon met others, climbing down. The mountain had become a regular thoroughfare, a highway to the clouds.

What brought us together so suddenly? The crowds merged into a line, a single line leading to the summit. I trudged along behind a party of five, matching my pace with theirs. They were slow. A third group overtook us and fell in step behind me. Streams of water trickled down the sandy trail toward Thoreau Spring, where a few people stopped to rest; they slid packs off their shoulders and squatted on the rocks. One man dipped an aluminum cup in the spring, pulling up a shallow mix of water and sand. The remainder kept walking, still in a line. Eventually the lead party noticed the crowd behind them. "We're holding up traffic," someone said. They stepped aside to let us pass.

Now that the fog had cleared, it was a warm, sunny Saturday. A large dome of atmospheric high pressure ensured fair weather and clear skies. I should have known better. There is no solitude on weekends.

America's forests have lost the hint of menace they possessed four hundred years ago when the pilgrim William Bradford cowered in the shadows of tall pines. He gazed at the coast of the New World and declared it a "hideous and desolate wilderness, full of wild beasts and wild men." To his eyes the forest nourished darkness and evil.

Today's trees are young and slender, leaning over the stumps of the old white pines. Logging roads are deserted, left to fade under grasses and shrubs. Predators in the wild have dwindled in number; perhaps a few hundred black bears remain. The wolves are gone entirely, save for a rare solitary beast that sneaks across the border from Quebec. If we hear the wolf's howl today, we mistake it for the whistle of the wind. Even moose and deer have grown less suspicious of people and do not mind their presence.

Thoreau noted the change and regretted it. He scribbled his thoughts quickly in his journal: "When I consider that the nobler animals have been exterminated here,—the cougar, panther, lynx, wolverene, wolf, bear, moose, deer, the beaver, the turkey, etc., etc.,— I cannot but feel as if I lived in a tamed and, as it were, emasculated country." Two lines later he added, "Is it not a maimed and imperfect nature that I am conversant with? As if I were to study a tribe of Indians that had lost all its warriors."

Our modern perceptions of wilderness, of nature, started with Thoreau. Simply by listening to the wind pat the leaves, then walking up the forested mountainside into the clouds—and writing a book about the experience—he suggested that woods had a use outside commercial lumbering. Anyone who read his *Ktaadn* travelogue, and the nature writings it inspired, learned that the woods

were a good place to canoe, to hunt, to pretend for a week that you
were a pioneer.

The Abenakis lost their fear of the ghost Pamola in the middle
of the nineteenth century, when herds of caribou were discovered
on Katahdin's tablelands. Taboo or no taboo, that meant good hunting. White hunters also made the discovery, and soon those Indians
who did not go as hunters went as guides, or merged the two jobs
into one. There had been caribou—and in all likelihood Abenaki
hunters—on the packed snow of the upper reaches for hundreds of
years, but rifles and the popularity of hunting for sport and meat
thinned their numbers with new efficiency. Sometime in 1903, a
hunter stood on Mount Katahdin and shrugged. "Seen one caribou, you've seen 'em all," he said. And then he shot it.

That same year, the journal *Appalachia* issued this epitaph: "The
caribou is an animal of the past in the Katahdin region. Today
all that remains is its bones in the porcupine dens." In the Great
North Woods the animals faced extinction; they retreated to regions closer to the pole: Canada, Alaska, Greenland. They have
never come back to stay.

An alpine plateau like Katahdin's doesn't seem a likely place for
caribou or moose or any large mammal. The mountain looks like
a boulder-strewn piece of moonscape, somehow misplaced during the creation. Surely such a desert was never meant to harbor
life? A hiker in the 1920s, noting the bleakness of the land among
the clouds, said, "This is where herds of caribou roamed in former
years. So they might, if able to eat and ingest granite." But caribou
did indeed inhabit the snowy tablelands.

Three attempts were made to restock the North Woods with
caribou—programs as uncertain, if not quite as controversial, as the
reintegration of wolves in the West. They have failed. The Baxter
State Park Authority approved two attempts to reintroduce caribou in the 1960s and the late 1980s. Several of the caribou wandered out of the park toward the Quebec border. Bears killed four,

coyotes two, and at least one plummeted to its death off a rock cliff.
Others succumbed to disease. Park authorities rejected a request
for a third attempt in 1990. A private organization called the Maine
Caribou Project released about twenty of the animals just outside
the eastern boundary of Baxter State Park. The caribou staggered
away. None survived.

Opinions varied as to why the animals "stubbornly" continued
to die. One veteran forest volunteer pointed out that caribou are
sometimes solitary animals. Released in small numbers, they might
drift apart and never meet again to mate. But history tells us that
they also herd together—and so are easier to hunt, not just by humans but by bears, coyotes, and wolves. There is probably some
truth to both theories. Caribou herd, but the females separate
to give birth and thus become vulnerable to hungry black bears.
Baxter State Park's 1990 Annual Report suggested that at least one
hundred caribou would need to be released together "to offset predation and other mortality factors."

Even if they do escape the claws and teeth of bears, disease will
still bring them down. Brainworm, a parasite carried by deer, is what
has kept the Katahdin region permanently free of caribou, just as it
holds the moose population in check. Deer suffer less from the parasite, but they spread it through the woods. Snails crawl across deer
droppings thick with brainworm larvae, then ooze up plant stems
where they are ingested by grazing moose. Any moose unfortu-
nate enough to eat grasses sullied by deer scat will die. Sadly, many
moose who unexpectedly journey to odd places—like the streets of
Boston—and thus make an appearance on the evening news are vic-
tims of the deadly disease. Addled and confused, they are quite unaware of their brief celebrity and soon die. Caribou are even more
susceptible than moose, and attempts to bring back a mere dozen
or so animals never stood much chance of success.

In the past, natural predators kept the deer population in
check, and brainworm—*Parelaphostrongylus tenuis*—did not much

trouble moose or caribou. Now, protected inside the wildlife refuge of Baxter State Park, deer flourish, moose endure, and caribou inevitably perish. "Deer and caribou don't mix well," says Jean Hoekwater, park naturalist. "We're not going to decimate our deer so they can release caribou."

The last frontier in the eastern United States is the North Woods, a patch of wilderness under siege. Like Alaska, its cousin in the northwest, much of the rural woodland lacks towns, paved roads, or electrical wires strung in lines over the trees. There are few automobiles, since it is easier to fly across than to cross by land. Roads that do exist are logging roads crowded with trucks, each trailer hauling timber south to the mills where it is ground into pulp for paper towels and the *New York Times.*

Unlike Alaska, this pocket of forest is small, a day's drive from New York, New Jersey, and the collection of villages wedged into the lower half of New England. Forty million people inhabit southern New England, in crowded towns and shrinking farmlands. A vein of traffic connecting this throng to the North Woods is never far away. The east-coast thruway, I-95, funnels cars full of tourists just forty miles past a cluster of old-growth hemlocks that has never felt the ax.

Occasionally a wild animal strays and sets a paw or hoof on the strips of pavement that we humans have laced through the trees. Once, when I was on my way to an appliance store in the city of Bangor, I saw a bull moose step across I-95. As he loped across the highway in five or six strides, the bulky "Adam's apple" under his chin bobbed up and down like a half-swallowed grapefruit.

Later that night, I drove in my rusty Oldsmobile from Maine to Massachusetts, worrying about the dangers of hitting a moose. Far in the north, a spatter of starlight was visible around Polaris; elsewhere, the sky was blocked by trees and clouds. All the way from the

Millinocket exit to Augusta, the sixty-five-miles-per-hour highway was moose country, a virtually endless swath of trees—boring and sometimes deadly for late-night drivers.

My highbeams cast a pale glow on the blacktop. Nervously, I peered at the fringes of that halo of light, watching for moose, or deer, or any animal. The road was empty—for now.

As my lights uncloaked the dark road yard by yard, I stayed alert. There is no time to stop when a half-ton moose suddenly walks into your lights. There is only time to swerve.

By the time I reached the Massachusetts border, still awake and moose-less, I thought I was safe. I was wrong.

It never occurred to me to be scared. Not until hours later did I see images of crumpled metal and ruined fenders, or, worse, picture the animal's carcass slamming through the windshield, landing in a heap of blood and glass on my lap.

U.S. Route 202 is known as the Daniel Shays Highway, named after a farmer who led a ragtag army in rebellion against our fledgling nation during the winter of 1787. His road spans the twenty-five miles from Orange, Massachusetts, to Belchertown, tracing the western outline of the Quabbin Reservoir, which provides Boston's drinking water. To preserve the purity of the city's water, the reservoir is surrounded by tiny, undeveloped villages and a vast tract of woodland—home to a large population of white-tailed deer, but no larger mammals. Despite the occasional sightings of moose and bear in the Berkshires, I had never seen either one at the Quabbin.

As the seconds ticked by at four in the morning, the Daniel Shays Highway was empty, save for me. Although the speed limit was a painful forty miles an hour, I paid tribute to the rebellious spirit of the road's namesake and rounded a corner at fifty-five.

Instantly, a doe rigid with fright froze in the headlights' glow. Her sudden dash onto the road shocked me. I hit the brakes and slowed gradually—too gradually—while the tiny, rigid animal grew ever larger and closer. The needle on the speedometer swung toward zero.

At first, thinking there was plenty of room, I just tapped the brakes, as if I were merely gliding to a halt before a stoplight. Seconds later, that gentle pressure became a full floor slam. My body was flung forward, then caught and shoved back by the seat belt. A stack of books on the passenger-side seat toppled in a heap on the floor. A screech of tires. A brief, half-born panic.

And then the encounter was over. The car was still rolling at the pace of a fast walk when we connected. A tiny bump shimmered through the frame; the doe crumpled and folded up out of sight below the engine, like a child curling into a frightened ball. I waited. All at once she sprang and bounded out of sight, lost in the darkness of the trees.

That doe was surely bruised, terrified, her frantic heart squirting spasms of blood and adrenaline. But she was alive. I survived intact; my car suffered no new dents.

For a moment I groped under the seats for the fallen books, my foot still perched on the brake. Once again, I was alone with the road. A glance back in the mirror revealed the reddish burn of my lights mingling with a softer light: the first tint of sunrise, a dawn the doe and I were both glad to see.

So far civilization has tended to spill south and west with its excess population and recreational urges, but now it needs room and has remembered the lost pocket in the north. Pastures, meadows, and forests quickly fill with the asphalt lots of Wal-Marts and Pizza Huts. Weary city dwellers retire to the country for the quiet, the trees, the starlight—yet they bring along their urban attitudes. For safety, floodlights drown their patios, lawns, and driveways in a simmering ocean of electricity. Shopping malls spring up like mushrooms in the rain to accommodate the newcomers. Small towns quickly evolve into small cities; the bubble bursts. Don't people realize that they cannot escape the city if the whole metropolis moves with them?

"I don't know how people can stand to live in cities," scoffs a gruff, rural resident. "But thank God they do. Can you imagine what it would be like if they all left?"

I can imagine. It's happening. In the last century and a half our numbers have increased tenfold. In 1846, the year Thoreau made his first trip to Maine, less than a hundred people were known to have climbed, or even seen, a hillock like Katahdin. They were surveyors, geologists, and botanists—not casual tourists. In the days before written records began, perhaps a few hundred Abenaki climbed the mountain. That's all. Now nearly twice that number will stand in conquest on its peak in a single afternoon.

Gone are the days when a mountain climber took an ax to chop open a parking space alongside the logging tote roads. By eight o'clock in the morning on a Saturday, the parking lot at Roaring Brook campground is a hotbed of metal and glass, reflecting the sun. A sign confronts hikers at the head of the trail to Chimney Pond: "All hikers must register here." An arrow points to the porch of the ranger's cabin. On the back is another command: "All hikers please sign out before leaving." A short line of backpackers waits on the steps with their packs placed against the outside wall, since there is no room inside. The murmur of a dozen separate conversations fills the air. The registration sheet is already inked to its second page.

"It's steep!" a deep voice shouts.

Five cotton-clad hikers have gathered around the replica of Katahdin on display on the porch. It's made of plaster painted green; the trails are marked in red. The leader of the group is a tall, blond woman with a New Jersey accent. A Nikon camera on a strap is draped around her neck like a medallion.

"That's where we're going, Chimney Pond." She points.

"Where's the Knife Edge? It didn't look like that driving in."

"It can't really be that steep. We'd need ropes!"

"Well, if a seventy-five-year-old woman can make it up there, it gives me hope that I can, too."

"Yes, but she didn't make it back down."

Outside I throw up my arms in mock despair. "Why are all these people here?" Laughter, of course, is the only answer, since I have come with a party of ten.

"Some days the lot fills up even sooner," says a ranger. He jabs a thumb at the sea of cars.

Two hundred people sign out this morning from Roaring Brook, the starting-off point for the beautiful glacial graveyard of Chimney Pond. The trailhead is congested with backpacks and bobbing heads wearing bandannas, but the crowds tend to thin to a staggered line about a half-mile up the trail. People settle into their paces, falling behind or striding ahead.

One of the larger groups disappears around a corner, and back at the ranger's cabin there is a brief quiet. I can hear now the roaring water from the stream. The ranger walks over to the model of the local topography on the porch, waves a calloused hand vaguely at the spike of the summit. "A couple hundred people at Baxter Peak today, and to some that's not wilderness, but to people from New York or places like that, that isn't many people at all."

It isn't too many. Not really. There are places on earth—the beaches of Maine, for instance, or so-called wilderness areas like Yellowstone— where the entire population of Baxter State Park on any given day would scarcely fill a single parking lot. But a gathering of two hundred people on the summit of a tiny mountain? Why do they bother? How many birds can squeeze into the nest before the branch snaps and spills the straw?

Something in the human psyche has changed since Thoreau's day. He practiced—and preached—economy and simplicity, and this attitude gave him the luxury of time without need of wealth. It was, perhaps, a situation entirely unheard of before 1846.

In more superstitious eras, individuals sought out rawest nature for enlightenment. They starved themselves in the desert, meditated on high mountains, and challenged the elements. Today, we bring along picnic baskets to these same remote places. We drive cars up mountains and share the view with hundreds of strangers. Do we seek the same thing our forebears sought, a communion with nature? Perhaps we do, but we can't seem to bring ourselves to part with the comforts of modern civilization. We seek out enlightenment in automobiles, eating hamburgers and slurping milkshakes along the way.

Thoreau traveled to Katahdin with a notebook in 1846, but hikers today will carry a Notebook™ on the trail. In 1998, during his two-thousand mile trek to Katahdin along the Appalachian Trail, Dick Bailey lugged along a laptop computer. "I knew of Thoreau, of course," Bailey says. "I'm not a big one for living off the land or getting back to nature. When I hiked, I took a computer and cameras, 'cause I take a lot of pictures."

High-tech gadgetry in the woods attracts attention. He toted his computer on the strap of his pack, in plain sight. "There were a total of three people I met the entire trip who voiced some negative opinion," says Bailey. "Most people thought it was neat as hell. One guy I met was a CPA. He figured, hey, if he could take one of those out on the trail, he could stay out longer and still do his work."

Bailey accepted the crowds along the Appalachian Trail with good humor. "The idea that you can have this wilderness experience to yourself is kind of ludicrous," he says. "There are about four million people a year who use some portion of the A.T. They've got as much right to be there as you have."

But do they also have the right to bring civilization with them? "A lot of people say they go out on the trail to get away from technology and everything, and they don't want to see cell phones and computers on the trail," answers Bailey. "But they're still climbing into their high-tech tents and they're wearing Gortex and everything. They just have picked what they want out of the high-tech world and figure everything else should be left aside. They're not hiking in wool or skins. If you really wanted to get back to nature you'd hike au naturel."

Laptop computers are not the only hiking accessories that would have made Thoreau raise an eyebrow. Dick Bailey recalls, "There was a guy who did the trail one year with a tuba. And a lot of people will start out carrying a rock from Springer Mountain, Georgia, to put on top of Katahdin when they finish." He joked that perhaps Springer Mountain was losing elevation and Katahdin gaining elevation as a result.

I thought about the surveyor Floyd Neary and the mile-high cairn on Katahdin, and wondered if Bailey's joke was really so far-fetched after all.

Noon. It took me three hours of hobbling up the trail until I ran out of land and had nowhere to go but down.

On the summit, a boy reaches up to the cairn that supposedly pokes a mile high. He removes the top stone and shouts to his friends—a large crowd, a school group—"Look, I'm shortening the mountain. Now it's only 5,279 feet high!" In the din, he's barely heard. The group, adult chaperones as well as children, are loud, spread out, hollering to and at one another. An adult yells to the kid, "Get down from there!" The boy obeys. But he is quickly replaced; an assembly line of children circles the stones. Whose turn is next?

Somewhere a whistle blows a shrill, tinny noise. The school group—or perhaps two school groups, it's hard to tell—are not alone. Other hikers, in ones, twos, and threes, seek privacy among the rocks at the top of the Great Basin, high above the glacial detritus of Chimney Pond. The newcomers, too, dislike the noise. A small, wiry man notices the frown on my face and waves an arm at the crowd. He says, "You wouldn't think people like that could make it all the way up here. You'd think they'd stick to their video games and not ruin it for the rest of us." The muscles on his face tighten in anger; I imagine that I can hear his teeth grinding. He did not come here to witness this nursery in the clouds. What he came for, and what I came for, was to see the mountain, supposedly "forever wild." I make a silent vow never again to climb on a Saturday.

The little man sneers, implying that "these people" would enjoy a picture postcard just as much as the real thing. I nod agreement to fend off further discussion. The man seems poised for a philosophical debate, which I don't want. I sympathize with his sentiment, but obviously this crowd is not satisfied with just a postcard, because here they are. Why do they come? Is it, after all, for the same experience I came for? Is it merely a matter of degree? Who, exactly, are "these people" that I set myself apart from them, as does the angry man and a few others who withdraw from the pandemonium. Why should we be forced to hide behind boulders? We all seek solitude, hoping that the raspy wind will dampen the chatter of children.

It's pleasing to think that offensive tourists belong to a species quite different from concerned visitors—though natives of the North Woods must laugh at such a presumption. How easy it is to notice someone else's noise while throwing an apple core of one's own to rot on the rocks. There's no real distinction.

I've noticed that most people litter and don't seem to care. This morning, I saw a ranger reach down to grab a candy wrapper off the ground. He said, "We seem to get less responsible visitors this time of year. We have to pick up after them more."

You would think such people would stick to other places, places already dirtied with litter, he laments. But they don't, or won't.

If, as the ranger claimed, most people lack the respect for nature that others would prefer them to have, then what draws them here? Why can't they be satisfied with Yellowstone's parking lots and hot-dog stands, or the snack bar and souvenir shop on top of Mount Washington? Baxter State Park doesn't seem the proper place to attract mountaintop diners or automobile hikers. Its regulations are too strict. "You practically need a passport to get in there in winter," grumbled a mountaineer who once was turned away; he had thrown his hands up in disgust at the quantity of paperwork and regulations. In summer, unpaved roads sink and rupture after any heavy rain, riddled with potholes. Cars creep along at ten, twenty, thirty miles an hour, depending on the condition of the roads. If they speed, they split a tire. There's no running water or electricity in any of the park's inner campgrounds, and for a majority of visitors it is their first experience using an outhouse. Pets are left at home, by law. The roads are narrow, so that at every turn—and there are many—cars in line nearly collide. Often the car ahead can be seen, felt, and breathed by the cloud of dust in its wake. Yet every year, more and more tourists infiltrate this park.

"There are people who come here who hate it," says naturalist Jean Hoekwater, holding up a glass of leeches—bloodsuckers—plucked from Nesowadnehunk Stream. "There's so few options available that this is where they end up coming. They'd probably be happier someplace else." The leeches go on display at Daicey Pond while Hoekwater talks to a group of children about the park's flora and fauna. Afterward—and she says this pointedly—the leeches will be released as close as possible to the spot where they were found.

As summer weekends grow older in July and August, and the days grow longer, larger and noisier crowds gather in wilderness parks all across the country. There are "so few options" because there are so many people seeking nature in a variety of degrees. Those who want nature served straight up—a minority—tend to resent those who don't mind pavement or cars or hot coffee to go. We often don't recognize that these people are on our side. Instead we feel that they come to ruin it for the rest of us—these people who feel a desire to see the trees but not necessarily to walk far amongst them.

Jean Hoekwater says that some people come to the wilderness expecting to find a garden. Off the sides of trails there are blowdowns—tall trees cracked open at the stump, revealing giant tangled masses of dirt, roots, and moss yanked up to dry in the sun. The rest of the tree is sprawled across the trail, clothed in heavy moss. "Sometimes people complain, 'Why don't you clean up the woods?' They look at this," she says, waving her hand toward the mossy branches, "and say we have a terrible mess here. I don't call it a mess. It decomposes this way naturally. This is nature."

Yes, this is nature, and there are people who want to tidy it up. Dig up roots in the trail. Chop fallen trees into cords of firewood, neatly stacked. Yet I remember fondly an adventure on Black Cat Mountain, where I stumbled across an entire hillside of uprooted trees. On that late summer day, it looked as if a tornado had wandered out of the Midwest and gotten lost, scattering trees in its wake. A mesh of overturned, leafy branches blocked the view. I was forced to stop, unable to find the trail. Nowhere was a blaze visible, or even a footprint. Puzzled, I laid a hand on the trunk of a fallen tree—and then jumped back, startled. Under my hand lay a splotch of blue paint—a trail blaze. The blowdowns hadn't simply knocked trees across the trail; they had completely destroyed the trail itself.

By a process of triangulation—guessing which way each tree had faced when upright—I worked my way through the blowdowns, back to camp.

It's alarming how small this wilderness park really is. Baxter State Park is less than half the size of Rhode Island, scarcely a speck of green ink on a map of the United States. Its size is likely to be its doom, for even if it stays protected, "forever wild" in the eyes of the law, the lands outside will ruin it. Smoke from the paper mill far below is always visible, a whiff of human progress, drifting closer on the breeze.

"It is in vain to dream of a wildness distant from ourselves," Thoreau tells us. "There is none such."

For now, the north country is largely a land of lakes and trees, and will likely remain so for years to come. On a ridge just above the Saddle Slide, a hiker stops and gasps in disbelief, "Where did all the lakes come from?" More and more lakes spring into view with every upward step, like blue eyes winking open. The terrain for a hundred miles in all directions is speckled with lakes, ponds, and streams, especially to the south. Thoreau noticed this profusion of lakes, seen through his yard or so of clear sun: "The forest looked like a firm grass sward, and the effect of these lakes in its midst has been well compared by one who has since visited this same spot, to that of a 'mirror broken into a thousand fragments, and wildly scattered over the grass, reflecting the full blaze of the sun.'" Who that later visitor was, he never tells.*

On a clear day, the woods and lakes extend forever. But almost none of what you see lies inside protected park boundaries. Gaze west from the summit of Doubletop, from the gravestone of Keppele Hall, and you are looking into paper-company land. At any time this wilderness could be logged or developed. Imagine a city like Boston where Millinocket is, someday. Thoreau's imagery would no longer be just a metaphor; there really would be a thousand windows scattered across the diminishing woods, reflecting the full blaze of the sun.

Already, development is a source of contention, tipping the delicate balance between people who hope to preserve nature without compromise, and others who want and need to make an honest buck. Condominiums appear. A paper company plans to build a road around a nearby lake, which it owns. The park itself may be protected, but stripped of its buffer zone of trees, perhaps the park

---

* Since Thoreau's day, a surprising number of authors have quoted, misquoted, and occasionally stolen outright this passage from *The Maine Woods*. The words have appeared in trail guides, memoirs, and magazine articles. But when credit is given, it is usually bestowed on Thoreau, not on his mysterious "one."

The lake metaphor originally appeared in the *Bangor Courier* in 1847. The author was a journalist named J. K. Laski. As the only layman on a botanical expedition to Katahdin, Laski chased squirrels, trampled grass, and started rock avalanches just to listen to the noise—all with a sort of innocent glee. He also wrote about lakes in the forest: "I thought of many similes—but can give you the best idea of it when I say that the scene reminded me of that represented by a splendid mirror broken into a thousand fragments and widely scattered over the grass, reflecting the full blaze of the sun."

The bulk of Laski's energetic essay is chock-full of exclamation points, dashes, italics, and wild similes. At one point he compares the Knife Edge, a mile-long glacial arête on the mountain, to "the nose of a big man." His original article was later reprinted in the *Maine Naturalist* in June 1927 and is now located in a dusty corner of the Special Collections Room at the Fogler Library at the University of Maine in Orono.

will lose much of its worth. The only regions with "pure" nature will sit in the bottoms of valleys, deep in the basins. Views from the heights will be lost forever.

The problem facing conservationists is that they can never be a majority. They must fight against a growing population that wants electricity, water, newspapers, jobs, and places to live. How can they deny people these basic needs? How can they force logging families to accept welfare rather than earn a living?

People also want a place to play, a place to get away from home and see the sights, a place to go fishing or to charter a boat. Conservationists encourage this up to a point, but they would rather that most people went somewhere else. The sheer numbers of weekend travelers make the places they visit resemble the places they've left. Spaces must be made for all their cars, and people must be fed and entertained. Near every park lies a small city of restaurants, stores, and motels. Tourism is the lifeblood of the city, but the city is a parasite to the park.

Conservationism demands idealism rather than realism. When it comes down to a choice between a place to live or a park to visit, the place to live will win. Mile by mile, civilization will need land, and it will take it.

What conservationists have to their advantage is a firm belief—not shared by all—that a crisis is coming and it's wrong to put off a resolution till the end. We can only delay the end, not stop it. Face the pain now, they say. Force a solution, and still have something worthwhile left over. Civilization is not the natural enemy of nature, just as the poor do not inherently hate the rich. Civilization takes what it needs because it cannot survive without. It has grown, like a plant in a pot, to the point where it no longer fits in that pot. Its roots press against the ceramic wall and coil inward, trapped. Its leaves spill over the sides, dangling listlessly above soil and minerals that the roots cannot tap. Who can blame the plant for breaking through the walls and finding a bigger home?

The problem is that civilization continues to grow, and as it does it demands ever more soil to grow in. This is fine—until we run out of soil. The way of life we have in America now demands power and food and homes. If we take more land and use it, we can continue the life we lead now, and put off till the future the problem of what to do when there is no more to take. But then, at last, something will have to give; life will have to change, whether we like it or not.

The conservationists' answer is to declare that moment today—Stop!—we have no more soil to take. Find the solution now, or, if there is none, work out a new way. There will be economic hardship, yes, and there will be change, but there will also be a natural world, fragmented but still available. It may only be for the few, but at least those few will still have it. Perhaps, like buying a car in Poland, or renting a parking space in New York, people must wait on lists for years before their chance arrives to visit a park. At least there will still be parks worth visiting.

In Baxter State Park, occasionally a curious visitor asks about the wreck of the U.S. Air Force plane that crashed into Fort Mountain during World War II. The plane's shell still rusts on the hillside, but its cargo—including the corpses of its eight crew members—was toted out of the woods by volunteers during a two-week salvage operation in 1944.

No trail leads to Fort Mountain. No camp exists nearby. The peak is reached by a difficult bushwhack trip down from the four-thousand-foot North Brother, itself miles from the nearest road. And yet still this obscure peak attracts visitors. When two men from Quebec drove up to the gatehouse at Roaring Brook in a rusty Volkswagen Beetle and announced that they planned to spend the night on Fort Mountain, Ranger Bob Howes told them no. Camping was allowed in campgrounds only.

Howes, the district ranger for the southern half of Baxter State Park, is a thick-set man, neither tall nor short. His close-cropped hair is blond, where he still has it. After working for more than two decades in the North Woods, Howes has built up a repertoire of stories—bear stories, tourist tales, quips about Governor Percival Baxter—and he delights in telling them. If asked, he will talk about bears for an hour, as if it's his duty to preserve the wilderness by storytelling; if he stopped for a breath, who knows what might happen?

Once, when I asked another ranger how much Howes knew of the rich history of this forest, this mountain, she replied, "He *is* the history!"

I heard his anecdote about the two men from Quebec told twice in one week. Howes said, "They were disappointed about Fort Mountain, and argued a bit, but finally asked where they could camp. There was a vacancy at Kidney Pond, so I sent them there. But I could see what they had in mind. I had a feeling about those two."

Later, near sunset, Howes checked up on them at Kidney Pond. "Sure enough," he said, "They never showed. So I drove out and found their car on the road at the base of the mountain." He sent rangers to wait by the car until the tourists wandered back down. "We were pretty sure they were camping out by the plane, though they might have been lost or injured." After a few hours Howes had the car towed; the other rangers left for home. "So now I knew they'd come looking for us."

In the morning, the two men did come looking. They walked three miles to Kidney Pond to report that their car was stolen.

"'Well, I can help you with that,' I said." Bob Howes paused, scratching his chin. "So fellows, what happened? You never showed up at your camp. 'We couldn't find it,' they told me. 'We got lost.'"

"Well, you found it all right this morning," said Howes, laughing softly at their weak excuse.

In many state or national parks, such an unauthorized night of camping either goes unnoticed or else results in no more than a parking ticket and a fine, if that. The only punishment is a verbal slap on the wrist. If you foolishly wrestle with bears, and survive, no penalty is issued except the swat of a paw. For certain offenses, the fines are payable by mail. A ranger or police officer you never see sticks a ticket on your car and moves on. No one cares where you are, where you go.

Perhaps we should care, or soon must care, as our own numbers grow. Perhaps the crush of travelers in wilderness areas soon will make us care. In alpine regions, in guidebooks, and on signs, hikers are urged to stick closely to the trail—not to keep from getting lost but to avoid killing plants. Hikers tend to stray a few feet from the marked trail. As a result, a wide, worn strip runs up the mountainside; mosses, lichens, and rare alpine vegetation perish under the impact of too many boots. Above timberline, where the arctic grasses are especially fragile, the trail may stretch forty feet across.

Signs and admonitions from rangers do little to prevent the problem, but at least not all parks have been forced to resort to the tactics of Yellowstone or Acadia, where the grass is buried under cement to stop people from walking on it. In Acadia National Park, a paved road—hailed on certain travel brochures as "the most scenic road in America"—winds around Cadillac Mountain to a parking lot on the summit, overlooking the blue dunes of the ocean. There are also foot trails for the relative few who prefer to sweat to earn their view.

By contrast, nearby Baxter State Park supports preservation before recreation. The perimeter road is not scenic at all, but a bumpy, twisting, dirt path. Sometimes, almost by accident, it offers a view of Katahdin or the cheese-shaped wedge of Doubletop or lower hills, and there are a few places for sightseers to pull a car over onto a gravel shoulder. But Percival Baxter meant for us to enjoy his park in the open air, not trapped inside the metallic shells of automobiles. He wanted "small cabins for mountain climbers and those who love the wilderness . . . only trails for those who travel on foot or horseback, a place where nature rules." In 1937 he wrote a snappish letter to Senator Frederick Hale of Maine: "If the Federal Government wants to establish a National Park in Maine they have twenty million acres other than Mt. Katahdin from which to make a selection."

Late one night I was driving alone toward a camp on the outskirts of Baxter Park when a fox dashed in front of my car. In the glare of my headlights, her coat glistened like a brush stroke of brilliant red. She stared into the deadly lights and stood her ground, straddling the broken gravel. Her fur trembled, ruffled by wind, and a spark of defiance burned in her eyes. Could I stop in time?

I nudged the brake pedal with my foot. Closer, closer—and at last the fox panicked, darting into the shadows of the pines.

A tightening noose of logging roads constricts around the North Woods, while suburbs and shopping malls intrude from the south. Across the United States, we already fear that our parks are over-crowded. We think that the sunset in the hills somehow will look pale and diluted if shared with too many people jostling our elbows. An investigative series run by a local newspaper in 1991 asked, "Are we loving our parks to death?" It seems we are; or if not loving, then certainly using them to death.

A cluster of wilderness enthusiasts known as "RESTORE: the North Woods" is trying to turn the tide, to wall up the dam. Few people who live in the area in question know anything about them, except perhaps to snort in disgust when told of their plans. There is no alliance between the environmentalists and Baxter Park. "We keep our concerns in house," rangers say. "It's our duty to protect Governor Baxter's gift." What an outside group like RESTORE or the Sierra Club does or might do is not their business. Nor do they have any influence over the paper companies. One ranger says, "For the most part they've been good neighbors, though it's obvious we have a different mandate. We have to learn to deal with them fairly and practically." Because the view from Katahdin looks over clusters of old growth hemlock and other lands owned by paper companies, a messy logging operation would be plainly visible from the trail. "We hold this area very dear to our hearts," says Jean Hoekwater. There is an annual meeting scheduled, she tells me, between park officials and paper company officials. But the company owes nothing—no explanations or apologies—to the park or to frustrated environmental activists from faraway states. "They're a private business," she says. "They have no reason to publicize what they're doing anymore than you would publicize that you're going to mow your lawn."

"RESTORE: the North Woods" worries about that. RESTORE hopes to protect millions of acres of woodland surrounding what is now Baxter State Park; in doing so they would create one of the largest national parks in America. An impossible dream. I wish them well. A spokesperson for the project, James St. Pierre, claims that tiny Baxter Park is in danger of becoming "an island in a sea of mismanaged forest." He also has proposed a shuttle-bus system to relieve the traffic problem inside the park. This is the plan: A bus picks you up at the Togue Pond entrance and takes you where you want to go. It's a good, simple idea, but flawed: Where are we going to park all those cars? The lots at Roaring Brook, Kidney Pond, countless campgrounds—necessary evils—will merge into an enormous metal junkyard at the gate. We might as well stay in Yellowstone.

The philosophy of conservation is exactly what its detractors accuse it of being: selfish. True conservationists want what everyone else wants—to see the rolling blue hills blacken with shadows at dusk, while the sky glows red—but without the blacktop roads, parking lots, and restaurants. They can have such solitude and wildness only if no one else does. Nature, they say, should be saved for the few, for those who like it best. They believe it should be saved even if they themselves never get to see it or must participate in a lottery and wait for a vacation spot. Otherwise, they warn, it will be saved for no one at all.

Roads and trails cut thin veins through the woods, and along these veins people drive, hike, work, and play. Any patch of trees visible from a hotel window is mere decoration, not wilderness. Percival Baxter said, "I want pleasant foot-trails built and attractive camp-sites laid out in the valleys, by the brook and on the shores of the waters. Sites where simple forest lean-tos and small log cabins are available for those who love nature." A promising vision for any park.

Electricity and running water are fine, the conservationists say— in thunderstorms and streams. Baxter Park lacks toilets and electric lights. One night, while working as a volunteer at Kidney Pond, I scooped up a bucket of dishwater, carried it to the sink in the kitchen, and only then noticed a red bloodsucker swimming laps around the dirty plates. "Anybody want to help with the dishes?" I asked, hopefully.

Despite these inconveniences, the area still receives thousands of visitors per year—and this is nothing compared with the two to three million who annually bury Acadia or Yellowstone or the Grand Canyon.

What is it that makes people want to share a beach or a mountain with a conglomeration of strangers? How will people react when their parks and beaches fill to capacity and start to turn them away?

Does nature still satisfy crowds in search of solitude? Can crowds and wilderness coexist? In just one small park I've watched the debate flicker. I expect the argument soon will catch fire and spread from state to state. As crowds gather and ever more seek out the mountains and the trees, it becomes tempting and convenient to disregard the phrase "forever wild." Mount Katahdin is just one small environmental island, a tiny peak among many, but the waves of industrial development still batter against its shore.

Changes will be made, questions asked, solutions sought. It's a national conundrum, played out on local stages like Baxter State Park. What harm could it possibly do to pave the narrow Nesowadnehunk tote road here or there? It's only one road. It already exists. A black-top alley winding through the trees would keep down the dust stirred up by tires and allow for faster travel. I doubt the moose would mind; why should we?

Building additional campgrounds—wrenching open small patches of forest canopy—might relieve the pressure of too many tourists, for a while. Parking lots could be expanded—just a little—to permit more day-trippers to use each park. There have been increasing requests for modern conveniences like plumbing and electricity. Gas stations and restaurants could easily be added along the periphery without detracting much from the "pure" wilderness at the center of the park.

The pressure for development, for modernization—which some consider improvement—is growing. Percival Baxter expected all these changes. If he were alive, he would consider them all and pass judgment. Perhaps he expected new campgrounds to be built as people visited his park in increasing numbers. Maybe he felt sympathy for the civilized modern mountaineer who instinctively tries to pull the chain in an outhouse. As it is, we can only guess at his plans.

I think, in the end, he would have opted for compromise. If the people—his neighbors—needed to cut trees to stay off the dole, Baxter would have bought them all chain saws and stood aside with a tear in his eye. If his neighbors were starving, he would have permitted the hunting of moose.

Idealists are undoubtedly distressed by this opinion. Realists, I hope, are befriended. Perhaps, out of sympathy, they will spare a few pockets of wilderness during the ongoing devastation of our remaining forests.

"While I am living," Baxter said, "I fear no encroachments on the Park, but as time passes and new men appear upon the scene there may be a tendency to overlook these restrictions and thus break the spirit of these gifts."

In the early half of the century, Teddy Roosevelt was troubled by the same concern; he stood at the edge of the Grand Canyon, shoes red with the dust of desert sand, and uttered a warning for the generations to come. "Leave it as it is," he said. "You cannot improve on it. The ages have been at work on it, and man can only mar it. What you can do is to keep it for your children, your children's children, and for all who come after you."

Roosevelt's image is carved high in Mount Rushmore, his scowl sketched forever in stone. But no thoughtful or beseeching eyes watch us on Katahdin as we scramble up the granite slopes. High on the mountain, the only faces we see are our own.

Memories

Human memory is fickle, unpredictable. I've learned not to trust it. Our memories form a tapestry that frays over time; the holes are stitched back together with nostalgic fictions and wooly truths, until who knows what really happened?

All of what I remember about an autumn trip to the North Woods cannot possibly be true. Too many gaps exist. What I remember most vividly is misery. The straps of a fifty-pound backpack cut deep trenches into my shoulder blades. Each step was another cut of the saw. The belt strap refused to transfer the weight to my hips, where it would be easier to haul. The weight compressed my vertebrae, squeezing the bones like an accordion, so that by sunset I fully believed I stood at least two inches shorter than at dawn. A pair of boots bought for forty dollars chewed raw the skin along my heel. A passing hiker saw agony written in the lines of my face and joked, "The Sherpas should be here any minute now."

The Sherpas never came. What arrived instead was rain. Cold droplets struck the mat of fallen maple leaves with a constant dripping, popping sound. A wet cotton shirt clung uncomfortably to my back and chest until I peeled it off like a label and replaced it with wool.

It rained all day. My joints ached, my knees throbbed. But piercing the grim moments was a surprising joy. A momentary shaft of sunlight cut through the clouds. I strolled down (or more often, up) the trail, breathing rich, fresh air. Pain in my feet and shoulders faded to a dull ache; willfully I choose not to stop. The swirling winds embraced me.

My walking stick is not elaborate—just a long, thin branch that happens to be of perfect length. Someone kindly left it propped against a sign at the head of the trail, available for the next hiker to pass by. As it happened, that hiker was me.

I walk to the edge of Roaring Brook and sit. Depending on the amount of rainfall or melting snow, the water roars, murmurs, or gurgles. As the seasons change, so does its volume. The brook has talked without a single pause since the time the last glacier melted on the shoulder of the mountain, thousands of years ago. Now cold, clear liquid strikes at the rocks in the streambed with a percussive slap.

On the far bank, a narrow crust of ice juts from the boulder where my friend Jenn sits, waiting.

The two of us are alone. The woods are quiet, empty. Though we know the earth is just asleep, hibernating, it feels dead. Animal tracks—bear claws, hooves of deer and moose—press like fossils into the dry mud of October. Over these cavities stand ghostly silhouettes—outlines of empty air.

My friend discovers a dragonfly perched on a rock, still and cold. Perhaps it is dead. She touches it, picks it up. The wings suddenly twitch. The insect squirms. She lets go, and we watch the insect flutter back to the rock and lie motionless again. The numbing cold holds it down. Soon not even the insistent prodding of the wind will cause it to live again.

The dragonfly makes me wonder. What vital ingredient leaks away in the second between life and death? Where does it go? Deep inside that husk of insect skin, etched into a coil of DNA, is a recipe for dragonflies, a recipe four billion years in the making. The instructions compel the dragonfly to grow, to eat, to reproduce. The insect's body is draped loosely around its genes like a coat. The animal itself is just a skin to shed, a temporary shell, a scroll upon which its recipe is written. In the end, only its genes will survive.

Months will pass, fall and winter will yield to spring, and buds blossom into leaves. Bears and hibernating mammals will stagger from their dens, bleary eyed and ravenous. My friend and I will emerge from our cocoons of scarves and winter jackets into the warmth of spring. At our feet, maple seeds will sink at last into the fresh-thawed mud, slowly giving birth to new trees. But a lonely husk of dragonfly lying on the stones will never rise again.

I take a step across the trail, and suddenly a grouse explodes off the forest floor in front of me like a jack-in-the-box with an oversensitive spring. The bird takes refuge in the branches of a scraggly pine.

We see no other living creatures all afternoon. The weather has driven them into their dens.

"Weigh station: Place packs here." The instruction is painted on a wooden plank, nailed to a birch tree. Behind it, a peculiar set of scales hangs. I read the rest: "These scales were set by a certified fisherman." It is signed: "Will B. Dunn."

The place is Russell Pond, nestled in the heart of the mountains. The two swinging metal scales are the first manufactured objects to greet campers after a rugged seven-and-a-half-mile hike from Roaring Brook. Clearly, this isn't Rome; no roads lead to Russell Pond.

A northerly breeze skims moisture off the pond's surface. A bull moose stands in the water on the far shore, chewing lily pad roots for lunch.

Reluctantly I wrench my gaze back to the scales. My backpack, stuffed with tent pegs, a soggy cotton sweater, and enough food for three days has dug into my shoulders. Now I can fling it off. I feel weightless. Joy! I step toward the scales, snapping a twig underfoot, and suddenly another wild grouse erupts in the shrubs. Its wings squeak like gears in need of oil. They flap in terrified fury until at last the bird reaches the lower branches of a pine tree and glares down at me.

My friend and I drop our packs and weigh them. That's what the scales are for—to see who's toted the lightest load. The loser, we decide, gets to carry the tent on the way back.

The next day I discover that the tent doesn't weigh so much, after all.

"Strangers on the Confetti Trail" is the title my friend thought up for this essay, long before it was written. She probably intended to write it herself. I'll use the title anyway. The fallen leaves do make a colorful confetti, and we met our share of strangers—mostly grouse and moose.

Jenn thought of the title at night while we were playing gin rummy by flashlight in a lean-to that opened toward the water. Carib-covered peanuts served as poker chips. We both kept eating our profits.

A tangy smell rose off the nearby pond. Coyotes barked and howled on the distant shore. Just as I slipped into sleep, something large splashed in the water. A fallen boulder? That is my last conscious thought. The next morning, a ranger announces that moose were fighting in the pond at night.

Moose outnumber people here, but the number of people is increasing. Just twenty years ago when I came to Baxter Park as a child, the streams and ponds were clear and pure, and everyone I saw drank the water untreated. No longer. Today, fear of parasites and disease has added iodine tablets and water filters to the list of essential camping supplies.

Before breakfast, Jenn and I fill—and treat—our water bottles in front of the ranger's cabin. "Don't you wish you could trust water in the wild?" she laments. Her stove brings a pot of pond water to a boil.

The balding, middle-aged ranger on duty shakes his head. He informs us that sufferers of the disease have come to Baxter Park along the Appalachian Trail, though no cases have occurred at Russell Pond. Then he admits to drinking water straight from the tap, untreated. "Officially, I have to tell you the risks," he says. "But unofficially, I'm drinking the same water you are."

I fill my canteen.

A short, white-haired woman speaks with vigor: "I haven't been up this way for forty years. That was back before it was so damn regimented."

She swaps stories with the ranger about bears and the tricks they pull to steal campers' food. "They had what they call a kamikaze bear, a sort of adventurous, teenage-type bear," she says. Even when campers hung their food sacks high off the ground, on a rope strung between the trees, the agile bear simply climbed up and dived down at the sack, claws outstretched, tearing it free. The woman makes a swooping motion with her hand to illustrate the plunging bear.

One clever mother bear thought up a new technique. She hoisted a hungry cub on her shoulders, and the cub pulled down the food bag.

"Years ago, when bears first started raiding campground dumpsters, people thought it was a tourist attraction," the storyteller says. "Families would sit and watch. They set up benches." By the time the authorities realized there was a problem, the well-fed bear population had doubled. The rangers started to guard the trash, sealing the cans, making them inaccessible. "What they were left with was a bunch of hungry bears. And that's when the trouble really started."

Jenn and I encounter no bears at Russell Pond, but smaller animals visit our lean-to. A chipmunk perches on hind legs on the lean-to's wooden beam, looking at us. We have stacked our boots, wet and soggy from yesterday's hike, on the beam. We now sit barefoot atop our sleeping bags in the dry interior. The chipmunk appears suddenly, poking up its head, as if it had been hiding in my friend's left shoe all along, a tiny stowaway. The chipmunk soon decides we are harmless; neither of us move.

The animal suddenly launches up into the lean-to; perhaps it hopped, but neither of us saw it pass through the air, so quick was the jump.

The chipmunk fidgets and runs from bag to bag like a child let loose on Christmas morning. It sniffs inquisitively and soon discovers the little pouch where I've stored a mix of raisins, nuts, and chocolate—energy food for the hike. Just two inches from my knee, the tiny animal rears up on hind legs and tries to gnaw through the fabric. I hold still; an urge rises to reach over and pet it, as if it were a puppy or a kitten. I resist.

At last the chipmunk darts back to the beam and vanishes. Apparently this was just a scouting expedition. "It's thinking, gee, I better remember this place for later," says Jenn.

The next morning, we discover that the chipmunk has helped itself to an apple overnight. We find tiny tooth marks in the fruit.

I walk down to the pond, where a group of ten to fifteen young men and women has gathered with shovels, poles, and saws. I hear a question: "What do moose sound like?"

The speaker is a man from Italy, tall and dark haired with a round face that looks ready to break into a grin. This is his first week in the United States; he speaks in heavily accented English. He, like the others, is a volunteer, here to repair and blaze trails. Streaks of brown mud run down his pants, his boots, and his pale arms—signs of a hard morning's work. For a moment he leans a hand on a pine tree, but quickly he recoils and wipes the sticky film of resin on his jeans.

So far, he says, he has seen no sign—and heard no sound—of moose. He sounds disappointed.

The park naturalist, Jean Hoekwater, blushes at the question and runs a slender hand through her shoulder-length brown hair. She is thin, thirtyish. Bulky, waterproof boots protect her feet. "Well," she starts to say. Obviously she does not want to imitate the moose call. Behind her, a breeze sweeps down Sentinel Mountain, skimming the surface of the pond. She glances across the water for a second or two, as if hoping a moose might appear and demonstrate.

Two loons bobble on the surface like distant black buoys. But no moose. "Well," she repeats. Again, a pause. She pleads, "Someone else must have done that for you already?"

There is no escape. The trail-crew volunteers, some from Germany and Italy, others from Scotland, Spain, New York, and Pennsylvania (all foreigners, as far as the native-born Mainer is concerned) insist on a demonstration; they sense good fun. The naturalist fidgets. Just moments ago she was fielding harmless questions about loons and bears, now suddenly here's a request to imitate the most ridiculous looking mammal ever to fall off the ark.

Moose are a giant, almost grotesque member of the deer family. Their designation is *Alces alces*. One of the watching rangers jokes that it is Latin for "moose moose."

Jean isn't joking. "Okay," she says at last, "but I don't want you to see this." With her hands, she covers her face and issues a moan, a groan, and a squeak all at the same time. The sound is like the rusty engine of a '75 Ford pickup trying to turn over in February.

Laughter erupts from the group. "That's the sound of a lovesick male," Jean says. Someone applauds. She adds, "The rutting season for moose starts in mid-September, so you all may get to hear that sound again."

Relieved, her duty done, she returns to the safer topic of loons, the sleek, black-and-white waterfowl that inhabit local ponds, put

there by the Audubon Society. Posted signs encourage tourists to
leave the birds in peace.

Red-eyed loons can hold their breath for roughly three minutes,
diving as deep as 200 feet without getting the bends—the painful
bubbling of nitrogen in the blood—if they can find a deep enough
pond.

Later I wade out into the pond, which dips down only 33 feet
according to the trail guide—even less if you count the foot or so
of deep sludge and weeds oozing between swimmers' toes near the
bottom.

The loons pay me no heed.

The road between Katahdin and my grandmother's house twists
and coils through the fir-filled forest. I grew up watching logging
trucks rumble along that road, carrying payloads of stacked trees to
the pulp mill. Sometimes when I drove that road a fox or a moose
would step in front of my car, bringing me to a halt with screech-
ing tires. But never once was I stopped by a traffic light. There were
none. The land was wild, free.

That's what I remember.

Pamola

A stream of hot muddy water spills down dry soil, collecting clay and taking it to the sea. Around the stream lies a desert, hard and lifeless. The sun ignites on the eastern horizon at dawn, rises to its zenith, and stays there. It bakes the land as centuries pass.

The stream thins gradually. Mud and clay stick together in clumps and settle, blocking the water's flow. For a while a moist line meanders through the desert, darker than the dry sand. But it soon fades, healing over like an old scar.

A continent shifts its weight and moves toward the north, where the air is colder. New streams surge to life. The landscape is still a desert, but now the desert is disappearing. Small groves of trees jut up through the sand, and creatures—the most primitive of mammals—lope along the riverbanks and drink. Murky waters clear. Deep down, the stream's bed turns hard and rocky. The water digs, and keeps digging, eroding the stones. At last, a long, pink strip of granite is revealed, gleaming. A mountain is born. Pamola opens his eyes.

He watches for a million years as green plants clothe the rocks, and he sees the bulb of granite, Katahdin, rising from the water, becoming a small hill, a place for Pamola to stand and survey the world. Rivers tumble from the north and fork around this hill, split like the wind. They dig away the soil and the weaker rocks, but Katahdin resists them, rising while much of the land falls.

Pamola is only a young spirit. He is full of joy, and eager to test his powers. He discovers he can summon snow from the north. For a while this amuses him; he crumbles boulders with frost, plugs rivers with ice, and saturates the sky with snowflakes.

In summer, when Pamola illuminates the blackened sky with lightning, the animals in the forest below tremble. In winter, his tongues of ice make the beasts flee south, beyond his reach. Pamola laughs.

Millions of years pass. The mountain pokes ever higher, and from its peak Pamola gazes across a widening ocean. He watches the enormous shadow of Europe and Africa pull away, growing dimmer with time, until at last the distance defeats him. He sees only waves.

Animals transform, taking new shapes, adapting to the advance of trees and the colder climate. He lets them be now, no longer interested in their fear. Instead, he observes them. He waits.

Pamola scratches open a cave high up the slopes and makes it his home.

The mountain has grown ever larger, taller. A forest of pine, spruce, and sedge conceals the rocks, growing all the way to the summit. Pamola can find no open place to stand; he sits in the branches of a sturdy pine on the highest peak, gazing across the ocean. Something is happening over there; he senses it. Something has changed.

Ice descends from the poles, though Pamola hasn't called for it and cannot push it back. As Pamola has aged, his strength has waned. Four times the great sheets of ice bury his mountain. The glaciers scare away Pamola's beasts, kill his trees, stop his rivers. For three million years he shivers alone in the cold, waiting. The grinding ice carves open basins, bowl-shaped valleys, in the sides of his mountain.

The peak looks smaller now, to Pamola's eyes, though it is also steeper, more rugged.

He sleeps while lichens and grasses return. During his nap, the last valley glaciers melt and drip out of the basins. Saplings grow again on the lower slopes, but still the high peaks are flat and barren.

The wait has been a long one, but now Pamola sees them—people. He had often looked east, toward the rising sun, when he first sensed them. But they surprise him, coming from behind the distant purple mountains where the sun sets. People are walking across his continent. He had expected them to cross the sea.

Pamola curses on the mountain, and the humans tremble and learn to fear him. At first he brews storms to amuse himself, but soon he finds he must scare the people away or else they will hunt his beasts, eat his berries, live alongside his streams. He lets them live unmolested to the south, but forbids any to climb his mountain.

Few challenge him. The people give Pamola a name; it pleases him.

Generations live and die. Then a new people comes—this time from the east, across the sea. The two tribes fight, and Pamola decides that the first people are his people, just as the trees are his trees, for they are fewer and do not trespass as often. The others are too quick for his eyes to see. He blinks, and they have built cities along the coast. He blinks again, and they have cut down all his trees.

Pamola thinks he should call the ice again, push glaciers down to the sea to remove all the people, new and old alike. He decides he does not like them. But his powers are weak now, and summoning the ice takes too long. The ice is too far to the north. Long before it arrives, the people will have overrun his mountain.

The humans see Katahdin, capped with snow. Four of the new tribe climb up, bringing along another, an Indian, to show them the way. The Indian knows Pamola is there. Pamola sees the fear in his eyes, but still he comes. The others do not know Pamola at all, and this angers him.

A second group climbs up his mountain, but Pamola has now had enough. He hurls down snow and screams. Half of the people stop and turn back, and Pamola laughs. But the others go on, and with them is one of the old people, one who should know better. The old one builds cairns of rocks on the tablelands, and Pamola understands—the piles of stone are markers to guide the people out of the snow. He tries to bury them.

The people arrive at the summit, and their leader has a machine, an instrument, meant to assign a number to the mountain. A sacrilege. Pamola wants no people prying into his secrets, and he renews the storm. One man slips on ice and is wounded. Limping, he escapes. Pamola traps the rest for a night without food, but come morning he has tired and cannot maintain the storm. The humans scurry down the mountain to safety. They have conquered Pamola's mountain.

A plume of smoke rises out of the woods—a mill. The mill is small but hungry; it eats trees. Trucks and tractors clear roads and haul away the tall white pines. Chainsaws snarl even in the Great Basin, and their noises echo off the cold, clear waters of Chimney Pond. Pamola hears. Half a century passes, and the trees grow back.

At night the red, blinking light atop the smokestack in the town of Millinocket is just visible from Baxter Peak. In daylight, the impact of humanity on the landscape is more visible. Cabins are scattered throughout the woods around Chimney Pond, and the tiny figures of rangers and hikers may be seen peering up at the summit and at the hump of land that hides Pamola Peak.

Sometimes storms lash out unexpectedly at visitors to Katahdin, and they shiver and suffer. But once they are safe at home, comforted by a warm fire, they laugh. "It's just old Pamola," they say. "Losing his temper again. An Indian god, I think."

Pamola has withdrawn deep in his cave. He sleeps. That howling at night—it's just the wind on the rocks.

Dawn to Dusk

As darkness yields to day, our eyes open. At first we see only dim shapes in moonlight: the outlines of trees, shrubs, and leaves. Starlight winks through cracks in the canopy. Mars is a small red light blinking on and off as it swings behind high branches and is eclipsed. Stars disappear one by one until only the kneecap of Orion shines brightly enough to remain, a dim companion to the red planet. Soon even Mars fades.

Long shadows spring from the tree trunks, fixing the last of twilight to the forest floor. As the sky brightens, these shapes stay black. Then comes an instant when shadows fade into a rush of color; fallen leaves turn yellow, red, green, and gold. Textures—ridges of bark, knobs on tree trunks—come suddenly into focus.

A fog buries the foothills of Katahdin and fills the ravines, but deep inside the mist a new light appears, yellow and red, the splintered rays of sunrise. Fresh color mixes with the cold gray, warming it.

Finally, morning reels the sun fully above the horizon.

The mountain, Katahdin, turns black, backlit by the sun. At this early hour we see only the shadow of what the mountain will become once the sun has climbed far above it. Blinded by the sun, we must turn our eyes away from the stars, the universe. We look in on ourselves and pull a blue cover over the rest of creation.

Nightfall rips away the mask of our atmosphere, and for a few hours our eyes range far and wide. Sunrise puts the mask back in place. The very air becomes visible, and we focus in on a single star, the sun. The rest of the universe vanishes. A blast of light snuffs out the subtle flickering of starlight. Planets disappear, the moon pales. Asteroids and comets fly by unnoticed. No such thing as a galaxy appears in all the blue sky. Instead, there are cumulus clouds, cirrus wisps, sparrows, and jays.

A drop of dew clings to the fibers of a grass stem. Inside this globule burns a tiny reflection of the sun. This same image of sunrise multiplies across a single meadow, suspended in the still, clear water of a million beads of dew. Every stalk of grass holds a sun or two, gleaming red. A moose munching on a clump of grass in the morning feeds on these tiny flickers of sunshine.

All this is true, but scarcely complete. Our eyes may be open, but there is too much to see, too much to hear, and even more that is silent and invisible. An unfocused observer is overwhelmed with sensory input; he takes it all in and chokes on the enormity of the universe. The focused eye sees one thing only—say, a golden light reflecting off a shelf of rock on a high hill. He then gazes from rock to rock, hill to hill, but never reaches them all, or expects to reach them.

What can we do with a universe that is too big to see? Pick a single object—a forest, a knoll, a tree—and focus on it. But should we listen, or look, or try both at once? Is it possible to see the white-throated sparrow that sings at the first touch of dawn? Perhaps. But can we locate each and every bird that joins it in song? Hear every note?

Once we've watched the morning shift from blackness to sunshine, we think we've seen the whole show. It's like stepping into
the universe next door; behind us lies a shadowed, moody world,
in front of us is a land of light. The transformation is simple to see.
But do we notice the precise second when crickets yield to a growing orchestra of birds? Is there, in fact, a specific moment when this
happens, or do the crickets drift off one by one? When, exactly, did
the gibbous moon slip below the hills? It changed color just before
it fell—did you notice?

This morning the air is cold and clear. A golden red light cascades
down the ridges of the mountains. The tallest peak is still a dark
coal, but the illusion won't last long. As the sun rises higher, the
mountains once again transform into earthly brown hills.

The mountains due north and west of Katahdin show a different face today than when Thoreau boated past them in 1857. It was
his third and final trip to Maine. He marveled at the hills from his
perch in the canoe, but chose not to climb them. Even if he had, the
open granite summits that now entice hikers with their views were
absent then from all but the highest peaks. The forest fires of later
decades had not yet cleared their upper ridges of trees.

Except for one or two minor hills, Katahdin is the southern-
most peak in Baxter State Park. The little summits, the leftover
lumps, are so dwarfed by the bulk of this "Greatest Mountain" that
they are hard to discern. It's as if they did not exist. Nearby Rum
Mountain is loftier than any mere hill, but hikers wrapped in clouds
on the high Knife Edge don't even notice it, not even when it's in
plain view. "Where?" they ask. You point. "Where?" Instead of a separate mountain, all they see is a limb of Katahdin reaching down
into the woods. There is no Rum Mountain. It exists only on maps.

An even smaller peak, Sentinel—also called Mount Roosevelt
after the former president who climbed it as a college boy—is better known because of its isolation; it stands miles away from any

distractions, south of the cluster of hills over which Katahdin reigns. From an eagle's high aerie, Sentinel looks no bigger than a fold in the earth, a bump, but it's an unrivalled bump, so that on its summit we may find a view. Yet if the spirit of Pamola hoisted up this hill and dropped it in a heap of rock, dirt, and trees at the foot of any average peak in Colorado, it wouldn't be a mountain at all, merely the bottommost layer of a great ravine.

Europeans and those in the western United States, people who live under the brows of younger mountains, the Alps and Rockies, tend to laugh at what passes for a mountain in the East. They look at the ancient Appalachians and see lumps of earth covered with trees. Only naive people could mistake these for mountains. "Mountains don't have trees on top," they say. "Those aren't mountains, they're hills!" Perhaps. But the tallest of these hills, sharp with rocks and cold with snow in June, surely earns a grudging respect from any foot-weary hiker.

The Abenakis had nothing to compare with Katahdin and therefore praised it highly, hence the words *kette adene*, "highest land." Europeans were less daunted, and simply noted in their journals that it was, in fact, "a big hill."

Not until people began to climb mountains in earnest did they note its actual diminutive size and yet also its ruggedness and unpredictability, surprising on so small a peak. One hiker struggled over steep boulders on a twelve-hour trek from Roaring Brook over the serrated Knife Edge and down the Appalachian Trail.

"It's not big," she declared, "but it is."

There are certain things we go to mountains to find: sun, moon, sky. We seek the mountains to lift our spirits, to stand a little closer to the stars. Crisp air fills our lungs. Drowsy with cold, bumblebees sit like ornaments on the rocks. They exist elsewhere, but so, too, does everything else; it becomes too hard to focus. On mountains these things are pure, distinct, undisturbed, and isolated.

There's a wind that people go to mountains to find that cannot be found anywhere else. It's a wind we must scramble over boulders to experience, a wind that shapes rocks, dwarfs trees, turns soft rain into stinging needles. Climbers who reach the ridge suddenly find themselves unprotected by the great mass of earth they have walked on and are pushed back by the icy gale spilling over the edge.

The wind is alive, a spirited fluid, mischievous and ethereal. It twists and dives in great circles, swirls red leaves in small cyclones and litters them across the grass. It's a brisk wind that flings clouds out of Canada and hurls them to the coast. It tousles your hair, sends scarves flying out behind you. It keeps old snow chilled on the naked granite in summer.

When winter and spring yield to summer the air becomes vibrant. It can be seen, its many twists and turns traced by the motion of leaves and the quickly flying birds. It can be heard, wrestling with the trunks of trees or whistling through the cracks in cabins and lean-tos.

Mountain air is not meant to be still, dead, and empty, as on a humid, windless day in the lowlands. The alpine wind requires substance, filling itself with misty rain or snowflakes. Wind carries the scent of the spring thaw, and the smell of decay in autumn. It is never empty.

Wind causes the stars themselves to shimmer. Wisps of light penetrate our planet's atmosphere but are jostled on the way down. The atmosphere is always churning, gusting, changing density. A star's light refracts or bends, then bends again, and to our eyes on the ground the star appears to twinkle.

On the darkest of nights, perhaps two thousand stars are visible to the naked eye. Each star is a small, independent fire, filling the air with bright patterns, and these patterns in turn have filled our imaginations. For millennia we have gazed up at the stars and seen in them our own mythologies.

I remember a legend I read about as a child, in a book by Carl Sagan. The story described the night sky as a vast animal skin wrapped around the earth. Beyond this skin rages a great fire. But the skin is tattered and through its holes shine bits and pieces of the flame—the stars.

At night we see more, not less. The fall of darkness opens a window to the universe. Daylight is the time of blindness, of introspection, of tasks at hand. In the fierce glow of the sun our sight is restricted to the inner curve of the atmosphere. We can see the grass, trees, clouds, buildings, people, road signs—a million objects flash before our eyes. But we lose the distant galaxies, the planets, the phases of the moon, and the swirling dust of interstellar space.

Nightfall is a time when the lights are fewer and somehow more precious. It's people who pull the curtain on what night has to offer. We try to fight off the night with electric lights, but this only makes the darkness deeper.

In Maine, the later summer sun sets at eight, and then the shadows lengthen. In a cabin at the base of Katahdin, I light a candle. Years ago, I visited this cabin as a young boy. This time I am alone. Looking out the window I see only a reflection of the inside. The window has become a mirror. Beyond the glass the world is pitch black. I feel exposed, vulnerable, trapped in a weak circle of light. I extinguish the candle and suddenly can see.

There is light without electricity, light without fire. It's possible to mingle with the night, to see large shadows moving in the sky overhead and know these are the same harmless puffs of white wool that glide in daylight.

I have always seen cumulus clouds at night, when they are supposed to be invisible. Look up. Are there stars? If not, the sky is smothered with clouds.

Years ago, before the crowding of tourists made it unlawful and unsafe, it was possible to spend a night on Katahdin's summit, above the clouds, watching the stars.

The hardest part of mountain climbing is writing it all down. By comparison it's easy to straddle boulders in a place well known, or trace a route heavily marked with the footprints of those who have gone before. Wooden signs beg people to stick to the trails, partly to protect fragile plant growth but also to spare the rangers the chore of searching for stragglers at night. You're not allowed to lose yourself, to step on new ground. "Please keep off the alpine grass" says a sign that juts from the mist on the tablelands of Katahdin. Where one person goes, the rest will follow.

But the writer has no easy trail, no fixed direction, no footprints to follow. Writing is an exercise in bushwhacking. You carry a pen instead of a machete and cut a single, narrow trail through a forest of possibilities. The location of the trailhead comes as a surprise. You start with only a vague expectation of where you want to go—a trace, someplace high where the wind is cold and the view endless— but no clue about how to get there. Trees get in the way, thousands upon thousands of trees, shrubs, mosses, and ferns. It's impossible to describe them all; you must pick and choose.

Unless you are very lucky you will get lost, describe the wrong things, discover the bottom of the valley instead of the crest of the hill. Then you must decide—do you want to write about valleys or mountains? If the answer is still mountains, you retrace your footsteps, erase the digression, and begin again. No signs are posted to say this is the right way. No guidebooks describe convenient shortcuts. Not a single tree is dabbed with blue paint. You must find the trail yourself.

Every tree marks the head of a new trail. So, too, does every branch and every leaf. You can chose to follow the toad that leapt an instant before the drop of your boot, like a jumping box triggered by footsteps. Where will it hop next? With an ample supply of paper, ink, and time, you can try to redraw the mountain and all its inhabitants in detail. Or you can set down your pencil and pen, leave the stacks of papers disheveled on the desk, turn off the lights . . . and go outside, into the night.

Late at night, the mountain is a shadow. Climb it. Stumble over roots and boulders; bring along no flashlights, no candles. Rely on starlight and moonbeams for guidance. Follow the moon west till

you come to the brink of a cliff and can step no farther. There, on
the mountainside, wait for the break of day.

Hours pass, and fog settles again in the valleys. At last, somewhere
just below the horizon, the sun tosses up sprinkled, dusty light.

A sparrow sings, then golden flame illuminates the sky. One
bird, with an acuteness lacking in human beings, felt the first ten-
dril of light break over the hills, anticipating the rise of the sun.
Soon a second bird joins in, and a third and a fourth, and as the cre-
scendo builds, the air brightens.

It's summer now, but the woods clustered beneath Katahdin
smell like fall, dank and melancholy. Life is visible everywhere—
dewy grasses, flowers just beginning to bloom—but the feeling is
one of decay. This mountain is old. Every wildflower is a small petal
of irony, so briefly alive in an ancient, aging world.

The gusts pouring down the slopes are cold and alien; they don't
belong here in July. Katahdin does not belong here in July. It has
seasons of its own.

Epilogue

The scent of gasoline and spruce trees greets me at the Togue Pond gate. The sun's glare is blinding but the air is cold. My car's heater pumps loudly. Early morning frost, not quite melted, whitens the grass along the fringes of the road.

This is the southern ingress to Baxter State Park, and on any other calm, blue-sky day, here is where I would sit in line for who knows how many minutes, car idling and finally inching forward toward the ranger's booth. A uniformed ranger, eyeing my out-of-state plate, would lecture me on safety and the importance of not littering, then extract a nonresident fee. Or, if I were smart enough to borrow my grandmother's car, the ranger would simply wave me through with a smile, as if the lobster license plate on the vehicle was a certificate of backwoods competence.

Today there's no line, no ranger. This is not a normal day. It's the middle of May. According to an announcement in the newspapers, the park is open to the public for the first time since last fall. Campgrounds and tent sites are still closed—no overnight visitors allowed—but short day hikes once again are permitted in this most safety-conscious and strictly run state park. One rule: Get back an hour before sunset. Any stragglers will find the gate locked, their exit blocked.

I step out into the chilled air and peer inside the deserted ranger's booth. "Hello!" I call out. "Hello?"

Echoes answer.

Inside I find a lined notebook, open in the middle. The page is blank, but its purpose is obvious. I jot down my name and destination on the top line. Apparently I am the only visitor so far.

How quiet the park is now, compared with the hustle and bustle to come. In just a few more weeks, schools will let out, and vacationers from Massachusetts and New York will stampede north to see Maine's natural wonders in one long bumper-to-bumper line across the Kittery Bridge. But today I have the whole mountain—possibly the whole park—to myself.

Such an experience is a rare one, and I intend to treasure it. A hike to Baxter Peak is my goal. Standing on the summit of Katahdin, completely alone, is something I haven't enjoyed since . . . well, ever.

The selfishness of that thought alarms me. Would sharing the vista with a crowd of strangers really lessen the experience? Yes, I admit. For me it would. But why? Crowds or no, the glint of sunlight off the distant Atlantic still would be a thrill to observe. Glimpses of moose, deer, or bear would be no less a treat. Is this strange desire for solitude in nature a cultural trait, unique to Americans with our wide open, largely empty continent? The famous pioneer, Daniel Boone, eyeing the curl of smoke from a new homesteader's chimney several miles away, complained that the neighborhood was getting too crowded. So he packed his bags and moved west. Centuries later, the writer Bill Bryson, used to English walking trails that of necessity must wind and twist through and around villages and roads, calls Boone "an idiot."

Idiots or not, we Daniel Boone types do like our elbow room. The air is warming now; I roll down the car window and poke one elbow outside. My breath no longer congeals in clouds of condensation. I listen; the forest is silent. The only noise is the snapping of twigs under my tires as I drive at fifteen miles per hour down the washboard-riddled road to the trailhead. Naked, leafless trees weave a mesh of shadows across the forest floor.

My thoughts meander. How long, I ponder, could I stay here alone on Katahdin before I desperately wanted a hot shower, a warm meal, a change of clothes? How long before I would welcome the very things I've come here to escape: the ring of a telephone, the sound of another human voice? The answer, I'm embarrassed to admit, is "not long." A day on the trail, a weekend in the wilderness, perhaps even a summer of roughing it along the Appalachian Trail would lose their appeal if extended too far.

Such thoughts make me wonder if what I really seek is not wildness, but balance. So much of a modern life is spent sitting in front of a desk, a computer, a steering wheel. To actually stand up, inhale the brisk morning air, and hear the crunch of pine needles under one's boots is a refreshing change. We of the industrialized world spend so many hours boxed in, our only horizons the walls of the next cubicle or the aisles of the local supermarket or the stained-glass windows of a church. Do enclosures like these make us yearn instinctively for open spaces, wild places? Humanity has changed from barefoot hunter-gatherers to Nike-clad office dwellers, from riding on horseback to orbiting the earth in space shuttles, in a blip of geologic time. Perhaps our genes, our instincts, have not yet caught up. Could that explain the appeal of these occasional forays up mountains and past bear dens?

"Occasional" is the key word. I wouldn't trade my comfortable, civilized home for a lifetime in the wilderness, and I suspect

Thoreau felt the same way. He, too, sought balance, not isolation. How else can we explain his "chairs for company" at Walden Pond? Would Thoreau have hiked the Appalachian Trail, if it had existed in his day? Or would four months of walking without a single sit-down dinner at the Emerson's table be too much to bear?

Lately I've been asking myself the same question. (Not that I'm expecting a dinner invitation from the Emersons anytime soon.) I've often thought about indulging in a summer of hiking from Georgia to Katahdin. Not many years ago, that was something I was eager to do; today, though, it's merely something I wish I'd done. I wonder now if I'd number among the first-week dropouts that barely make it past Springer Mountain. Would sore feet and aching knees force me to pack it in so soon? Most likely I'll never know.

A week of wilderness and solitude proved more than enough for a boy named Donn Fendler in 1939. He arrived at the foot of Mount Katahdin as a typical tourist, a "slight, highly nervous, city-bred child," accompanied by his father, two brothers, and friends. They came to the woods with expectations of scenery and seclusion—the usual reasons. Within hours, the one thing Donn Fendler would be seeking was another living soul.

It was July, but fog veiled the peak, and Donn described the air as "cold and shivery." He and a friend, Henry, quickened their pace, eager to reach the summit, leaving Donn's father far down the trail. Thick clouds closed in around them. Henry wanted to wait for an adult to guide them back down. Donn, teeth chattering, was in a hurry to descend.

His first mistake was to give his sweatshirt to Henry, leaving himself with only a thin fleece-lined windbreaker; he wanted Henry to keep warm while waiting. His second mistake was not to listen to Henry, who told him he was being rash. The third mistake, understandable in the swirling mist, was to go the wrong way.

The trail vanished. Donn Fendler was not seen again for nine days.

Hundreds of volunteers mounted a massive search and rescue operation, and keen-nosed bloodhounds were even flown in by the New York State Police. The found no sign of Donn.

Twelve-year-old Donn had expected to meet up with his father and brother. Instead he encountered sharp, slippery rocks, difficult to scramble over, and "pucker bush" patches concealing deep caves. His feet kept breaking through the brush. The rocks slashed his sneakers; they were falling to pieces with every step. A mix of rain and sleet started to fall, soaking his dungarees. The wind snarled at him with a whining, sometimes howling, voice. Donn's mind conjured up memories of the stories guides tell children to frighten them around the campfire—stories of the Indian spirit Pamola. "He lived on the mountaintop," thought Donn, "right where I was standing, perhaps."

Donn slept fitfully that night beside a stream. The next morning, his pants were stiff and uncomfortable, so he threw them over his shoulder and carried them, hoping they would unthaw. His swollen feet no longer fit inside his sneakers. His stomach grumbled. Mosquitoes nipped at his skin. He waded down the stream, hoping to discover a campsite around the next bend.

No campsite appeared. Not that day, not the next. At night Donn curled into a tight ball, knees tucked to his chin, to keep in body warmth and expose as little skin as possible to the attacks of mosquitoes. He dreamed of ham sandwiches. By day he walked, slowly and painfully, on bare feet. When Donn shouted, only the wind answered.

I think about how different Donn's visit to Katahdin was from my own. Donn Fendler searched desperately for others. Me? I'm eager to avoid them. I hike steadily up the trail, basking in my solitude. A voice carried on the wind would disappoint me. Donn Fendler, not far from this very spot, probably wished for nothing more than an answer to his hollered "Hello!"

On the eighth day of wandering, a sharp rock sliced off the tip of his big toe. Donn felt nothing; he just looked down and saw blood spurting. He clamped his hands tightly around the stump of his toe until the bleeding stopped, then limped forward.

The end of his ordeal came on the ninth day. He spotted a camp, then canoes, then . . . people! A husband and wife named McMoarn at a small camp on the East Branch of the Penobscot River took him in. They fed him soup (his stomach could handle nothing else) and telephoned news of his rescue to a community that had all but given up hope. A doctor, Ernest Young, rushed upriver to the remote camp from Millinocket.

A relative of mine plays a small part in the story at this point. In 1939 my grandmother was a young nurse at the hospital in Millinocket. She packed Dr. Young's medical bag, just before he hurried off to treat Donn. "I would have been there if there'd been room in the canoe," she once told me. The only reason she didn't go was because the doctor was the size of a small elephant. Another body might have destabilized the canoe.

At the riverbank my grandmother handed Dr. Young his medical bag and watched him go. "He was so scared he was holding onto the sides of the canoe, sitting between the two men who were paddling. He was wearing a white, summertime hat. He weighed a ton."

Dr. Young didn't sink the boat. When he arrived at Lunksoos Camp, he met a wire-thin, moosefly-bitten, barefoot, pantless, shivering boy with half a toe, who was just glad to find company.

I try to imagine how I would feel after nine days, stripped of my boots and pack, missing the high-calorie peanut-butter-flavored granola bars and packets of gorp that have been powering me up the trail this morning. Would nine days lost leave me soft and civilized? Most assuredly yes. I love nature and solitude—just not too much all at once.

I don't intend to stay here for nine days. A few hours alone on Katahdin will be enough to satisfy.

Midmorning, I scramble up the Hunt Trail, the last leg of the Appalachian Trail, to the tablelands and finally to the summit where Donn Fendler's misadventure began. Donn took this same route to the summit, all those years ago, but the weather that greeted him was different, harsher. The wind today is calm. I sit on a granite boulder and watch cumulus clouds blossom along the horizon.

It's strange to have this mountaintop to myself. Well, almost to myself. A large black raven spreads his wings and arcs across the sky. He glides from peak to peak, Pamola to Baxter to Hamlin Ridge, riding the gusts—a trek that would take me all day on foot. The raven sees me, I know. Three times he darts directly in front of me across the gap of the chimney, and each time he caws twice. Perhaps he's saying, "hello, hello." It's nice to have some company after all.

Not too much company, though. Maybe the raven's cry means instead, "Go away! Go away!"

A sparrow abruptly flutters to a landing on the pebbles at my feet. She pecks at the ground, searching for any crumbs I've dropped— I've been munching on some homemade gingerbread from my grandmother's kitchen in Millinocket. But I've been too careful. The bird finds nothing to eat, and alights. With a spin of her wings, the tiny bird slides down on a current of air into the ravine, dropping three thousand feet in a matter of seconds.

I only wish I could reach Chimney Pond so easily. My knees always ache on the descent. But I'm in no hurry to leave yet. I could stay here all day. The mountain, for the moment, is mine alone.

I've always felt possessive about Katahdin, the peak of my childhood. It's as if I'd grown up here. Perhaps, if another human does show up, hiking up the Appalachian Trail, I should play Pamola and scare them away.

Is Pamola watching me even now? I wonder. The raven is back

again, swooping over the peak, past my shoulder, giving me what looks like a glare. Am I intruding into his solitude? How long can I just sit here, until someone else intrudes into mine?

Not long, I imagine. The peak is too popular, too accessible. I will have to share.

The raven cries again, then dives down into the basin, a black, feathered arrow flying swiftly over the white May snow.

ERIC PINDER has worked for many years in New Hampshire's White Mountains, both at the Mount Washington Observatory and at the Appalachian Mountain Club. He is the author of *Life at the Top* (Down East Books, 1997) and *Tying Down the Wind* (Putnam, 2000). He lives in Berlin, New Hampshire.

More Books on

The World As Home

from Milkweed Editions

North to Katahdin is a book in the
World As Home, the nonfiction publishing
program of Milkweed Editions dedicated to
exploring our relationship to the natural world.

To order books or for more information,
contact Milkweed at (800) 520-6455
or visit our Web site (www.milkweed.org).

Toward the Livable City
Edited by Emilie Buchwald

Wild Earth:
Wild Ideas for a World Out of Balance
Edited by Tom Butler

The Book of the Everglades
Edited by Susan Cerulean

Swimming with Giants:
My Encounters with Whales, Dolphins, and Seals
Anne Collet

The Prairie in Her Eyes
Ann Daum

The Colors of Nature:
Culture, Identity, and the Natural World
Edited by Alison H. Deming and Lauret E. Savoy

Boundary Waters:
The Grace of the Wild
Paul Gruchow

Grass Roots:
The Universe of Home
Paul Gruchow

The Necessity of Empty Places
Paul Gruchow

A Sense of the Morning:
Field Notes of a Born Observer
David Brendan Hopes

Bird Songs of the Mesozoic:
A Day Hiker's Guide to the Nearby Wild
David Brendan Hopes

Arctic Refuge:
A Circle of Testimony
Compiled by Hank Lentfer and Carolyn Servid

This Incomparable Land:
A Guide to American Nature Writing
Thomas J. Lyon

A Wing in the Door:
Life with a Red-Tailed Hawk
Peri Phillips McQuay

The Pine Island Paradox
Kathleen Dean Moore

The Barn at the End of the World:
The Apprenticeship of a Quaker, Buddhist Shepherd
Mary Rose O'Reilley

Ecology of a Cracker Childhood
Janisse Ray

Wild Card Quilt:
The Ecology of Home
Janisse Ray

Back Under Sail:
Recovering the Spirit of Adventure
Migael Scherer

Of Landscape and Longing:
Finding a Home at the Water's Edge
Carolyn Servid

The Book of the Tongass
Edited by Carolyn Servid and Donald Snow

Homestead
Annick Smith

Testimony:
Writers of the West Speak On Behalf of Utah Wilderness
Compiled by Stephen Trimble and Terry Tempest Williams

The Credo Series

Brown Dog of the Yaak:
Essays on Art and Activism
Rick Bass

At the End of Ridge Road
Joseph Bruchac

Winter Creek:
One Writer's Natural History
John Daniel

Writing the Sacred into the Real
Alison Hawthorne Deming

The Frog Run:
Words and Wildness in the Vermont Woods
John Elder

Taking Care:
Thoughts on Storytelling and Belief
William Kittredge

Cross-Pollinations:
The Marriage of Science and Poetry
Gary Paul Nabhan

An American Child Supreme:
The Education of a Liberation Ecologist
John Nichols

Walking the High Ridge:
Life As Field Trip
Robert Michael Pyle

The Dream of the Marsh Wren:
Writing As Reciprocal Creation
Pattiann Rogers

The Country of Language
Scott Russell Sanders

Shaped by Wind and Water:
Reflections of a Naturalist
Ann Haymond Zwinger

Milkweed Editions

Founded in 1979, Milkweed Editions is the largest independent, nonprofit literary publisher in the United States. Milkweed publishes with the intention of making a humane impact on society, in the belief that good writing can transform the human heart and spirit. Within this mission, Milkweed publishes in five areas: fiction, nonfiction, poetry, children's literature for middle-grade readers, and the World As Home—books about our relationship with the natural world.

Join Us

Milkweed depends on the generosity of foundations and individuals like you, in addition to the sales of its books. In an increasingly consolidated and bottom-line-driven publishing world, your support allows us to select and publish books on the basis of their literary quality and the depth of their message. Please visit our Web site (www.milkweed.org) or contact us at (800) 520-6455 to learn more about our donor program.

Interior design by Rachel Holscher.
Typeset in 11/14 Adobe Jenson Pro
by BookMobile Design and Digital Publishing Services.
Printed on acid-free, recycled paper
by Edwards Brothers Malloy.